BROADENING
YOUR BIBLICAL
HORIZONS

OLD TESTAMENT SURVEY
PART II: JOB–MALACHI

D0589705

by

Gary V. Smith, Ph.D.
Professor of Old Testament
Bethel Theological Seminary
St. Paul, Minnesota

EVANGELICAL TRAINING ASSOCIATION
110 Bridge Street • Box 327
Wheaton, Illinois 60189

This text replaces *Old Testament Survey: Poetry and Prophecy.*

Scripture quotations are from the King James Version Bible.

7 6 5 4 3 2 1
9 8 7 6 5 4 3 2 1

ISBN: 0-910566-47-X

CONTENTS

INTRODUCTION

Knowing Bible content and ways of communicating its truth are necessary for everyone interested in understanding God's revelation and ministering to His people. For this reason, Evangelical Training Association's equipping/training program provides courses covering both Bible and ministry-related content.

If you desire a better understanding of the Word of God and sufficient background knowledge of the Old Testament to minister to others, you will find this text, *Broadening Your Biblical Horizons—Old Testament Survey Part II*, of immense help.

This is the second of three survey texts. Its companions, *Broadening Your Biblical Horizons—Old Testament Survey Part I* and *Broadening Your Biblical Horizons—New Testament Survey* consider the first seventeen books of the Old Testament and the New Testament books respectively. Together the three texts provide a sweeping overview study of the entire Bible.

Here, in easy-to-read form, is a survey of the interesting and challenging Bible books of poetry and prophecy. To avoid duplication of historical background information, you will notice that the study is arranged in sequence according to the date the Bible book was written or when the prophet ministered, not in the order they appear in most Bibles. Also, to avoid specific differences in interpretation, the book simply presents what the Bible says rather than the various ways individuals and groups have interpreted some passages. For those who feel specific interpretations are necessary as well, we suggest that you consult additional sources. The bibliography found at the end of the text should provide you with more in-depth resources for gathering this information.

Thought-provoking questions, provided at the end of each chapter, help you rethink and crystallize the major truths presented and apply the teaching of God's Word to your daily life.

PSALMS OF LAMENT AND PRAISE

1

Psalms 1-72
Time Period: Approximately 1050-950 B.C.

The book of Psalms is somewhat like a modern hymnbook. Both are a collection of songs and prayers written by several people over a long period of time. Both describe the worshipers' response of praise because of God's power and love, their words of hope based on God's promises for the future, and their cries for God to rescue them from the troubles of life. Both collections of songs were used by believers in their private devotions as well as the public worship of God's people. Psalms were sung in the temple (Ps. 100:4—"enter into his gates with thanksgiving, and into his courts with praise") and by the early church (Col. 3:16 —"admonishing one another in psalms and hymns and spiritual songs, singing with grace in your hearts to the Lord"). When a psalm was sung ("Great is the Lord" from Ps. 48), the singer was testifying to God's greatness, the listener was hearing how God had worked in another person's life, and everyone was encouraged to trust in God's power. The psalms were filled with the emotions of fear and anguish because of persecution, as well as trust and love because of God's protection in the past. These prayers describe the close personal relationship that can exist between God and each one of us.

Many of the psalms were written to music, thus the heading of Psalm 4 includes the direction, "for the choir director, (to be played) on stringed instruments," or the heading to Psalm 5 has "for the choir director, for flute accompaniment." Psalm 3 has the word "Selah" at the end of verses 2, 4, and 8. This word means "to lift up," but it is not clear whether this referred to increasing the volume of the instruments or some sort of musical interlude. Several of the psalms encourage singing (Ps. 95:1,2; 96:1,2; 98:1,4-6) and others promote the playing of instruments while people sang the praises of God (Ps. 98:5,6; 108:1,2; 150:3-5).

The psalms were arranged into five subdivisions or books (1-41; 42-72; 73-89; 90-106; 107-150). This follows the fivefold division of the Pentateuch and may reflect the process of collecting these songs and prayers into Israel's hymnbook. Most of the psalms in the first two books were from David (3-41; 51-71), while many psalms in book three were written by Asaph (73-83). Songs of Ascent (120-134) and Hallelujah psalms (146-150) were grouped together in the fifth book. This suggests that the first two books may have been collected by David, the third and fourth by Solomon or Hezekiah, and the fifth by Ezra. The earliest psalm of praise is attributed to Moses (Exod. 15), but it is not included in the book of Psalms. The headings suggest that Moses wrote one psalm (Ps. 90), 72 psalms are related to David, two to Solomon and a large group to the Levitical singers Asaph, Heman, Ethan, and Korah (1 Chron. 15:16-24; 25:1-8). David appointed these Levites to sing and play musical instruments at the temple worship services. Some psalms were written while the people of Israel were in exile by the rivers of Babylon (Ps. 137).

In the New Testament Peter claims that David wrote Psalm 16 and 110 (Acts 2:25-35) and Hebrews 4:7 connects him to Psalm 95.

Historical setting

Many of the psalms have two settings—the original historical experience of the author who wrote the psalm (David out on a hill taking care of his sheep) and the later setting of the psalm as it was sung in the temple in Jerusalem on a feast day. Some headings suggest the original historical situation which caused the author to write the psalm. Psalm 3 was connected to the events surrounding David fleeing from his rebellious son Absalom (see 2 Sam. 13:34-18:33), Psalm 18 fits the context of David fleeing from Saul (2 Sam. 21-22), Psalm 30 commemorates the dedication of the place where God's house would be built (2 Sam. 24), and Psalm 51 was David's prayer after his sin with Bathsheba (2 Sam. 11-12). Other psalms contain no historical information about the situation of the author in their heading, but have clues within the psalm itself. Psalm 45 is connected to a wedding, while 27:1-3 pictures the author surrounded by evildoers, adversaries, and a host of enemies.

The people who sang these songs many years later in the temple services or in the early church did not always know the situation of the original author. Nevertheless, they could identify with the feelings of hopelessness portrayed in these songs because they had experienced similar emotions in their own lives. Other psalms were primarily written to sing the praise of God in the temple or at a feast day. These psalms frequently deal with universal problems or common reasons for joy that affect people in all cultures.

Categorization of the Psalms

The psalms can be put into several different groups that have a similar topic, structure, or use. There are messianic psalms (Ps. 2; 110), wisdom psalms (Ps. 1; 73), royal psalms (Ps. 96-99), Zion songs (Ps. 46; 48), and historical psalms (Ps. 105; 106). The next chapter will look at many of these different kinds of psalms, but here the most popular types will be examined: the lament and the hymn of praise.

Psalms of lament

People in Israel lamented and cried out to God for help for several reasons. Some psalms describe a situation in which the individual author or the whole nation is being attacked by some enemy. A city may seek for God's protection as an enemy army is marching against it (Ps. 44:4-16) or an individual like David might mourn his own personal situation when Saul had him trapped in a cave in the Judean desert (Ps. 142). At other times people lamented and confessed their sins (Ps. 51; 130), mourned because of a serious sickness (Ps. 6), or lamented the fact that they had been unjustly accused of some evil deed (Ps. 7; 17; 120). When people lamented, they frequently wept, fasted, and put on sackcloth and ashes (see Joel 2:12-17). These were not casual requests for God's blessing, but serious prayers because they did not have modern medicine, a strong army or police force to maintain law and order, or the money to fight someone who had falsely accused them. Their only hope was to depend on God for mercy and protection. The book of Psalms includes six or seven community laments and about 50 individual laments.

Most laments have the same general structure (our prayers also tend to follow similar patterns), although there is a good deal of individual freedom within these broad patterns.[1] The lament structure usually includes:

1. **An invocation, a call for God to help.** This is frequently quite short. In Psalm 13 it is "How long O Lord." The invocation is a recognition that the lamenter is turning to God for help. Indeed, God is the only source of strength for those who are having difficulty.

2. **A lament or complaint.** In this section the worshiper describes the problem that he is having. Frequently, three issues are brought up: God is not protecting them, enemies are persecuting them, and they are in sorrow. In Psalm 13:1,2 the worshiper complains about God in "How long wilt thou hide thy face from me?"; about the person's own situation in "How long shall I take counsel in my soul, having sorrow in my heart daily?"; and about the enemies in "How long shall mine enemy be exalted over me?" These complaints are honest expressions of how the people feel. They do not hide their feelings of sorrow or disappointment (God already

knows them anyway). Although they do not blame God, they do believe that God can solve their problems. They express their complaints because they believe their situation will change when God hears their prayers. In modern prayers, people frequently do not spend much time describing their problems or telling God how they feel about these difficulties. These psalms encourage believers to be open with God, to tell Him exactly how they feel, not to hide behind some sort of false impression or pious attitude.

3.   **A petition or request for God's help.** This portion usually asks God to listen to the person's prayer and act to bring salvation or deliverance from the problems of life. In Psalm 13:3,4 the petition is "Consider and hear me, O Lord my God, lighten mine eyes, lest I sleep the sleep of death; Lest mine enemy say, I have prevailed against him." Sometimes the petition includes the request that God would deliver from death, forgive sins, or defeat their enemies. The request is an admission that believers are unable to solve all the problems of life in their own strength. By calling on God for help, we confess our dependence on God and by faith rest in His strong arms.

4.   **Confession of trust or statement of confidence.** Even though believers may face great problems and feel very discouraged, the lament prayer is not a time to wallow in despair or depression. Once the petition was stated, the worshipers were to turn their attention from their problems to God, the solution to their petition. The confession of trust or statement of confidence was an expression of faith, an active looking forward to the fulfillment of the request. In Psalm 13:5 the psalmist proclaims "But I have trusted in thy mercy; my heart shall rejoice in thy salvation." Because the person believes God can be trusted, there is confidence that God's salvation will bring great rejoicing in the coming days. As the hymn "Turn Your Eyes Upon Jesus" says: "The things of this earth will grow strangely dim in the light of His glory and grace."

5.   **A vow of praise.** Many laments end with a commitment that the believer will sing God's praise when He has answered this prayer. In Psalm 13:6 the worshiper promises: "I will sing unto the Lord, because he hath dealt bountifully with me." What began as a burdensome lament, ends with a note of hope and victory, with the expectation of glorifying God and proclaiming His grace to others in song.

Some laments do not contain all these structural parts and others may contain two sections of petition or two statements of confidence. Each prayer is an individual expression that follows a somewhat unique series of building blocks. The people were different, the situations were different, and their sense of hope or hopelessness varied based on the seriousness of the problem.

A regular pattern of reading or praying based on the psalms of lament will help us to pray with power and honesty. God is interested in our problems and Hebrews 4:14-16 states that Jesus is anxiously awaiting to intercede for us at the right hand of God the Father in heaven. Prayer is a testimony to the importance of a personal talking relationship with God, our belief in the transforming power of prayer, and our desire to experience the joy of having our prayers answered.

Psalms of praise

Another large group of psalms are called hymns of praise. These fall into several sub-categories according to the structure, topic, or reason for praising God. Some hymns declare God's praise for answering the lament of a believer (at the end of the lament the worshiper usually promises to praise God for the answer to the lament). Psalm 9 is this type of declarative or narrative hymn of praise.[2] God is praised (9:1-3; 7-11; 14) because the worshiper remembers how his enemies were destroyed by God (9:4-6; 12,13; 15,16).

A second group of hymns of ascent were sung as pilgrims or regular worshipers were coming to the temple. They refer to the joy of seeing the city of Jerusalem and being in the temple to worship God (Ps. 122).

A major group of hymns proclaim the glory of God and list a series of reasons why God should receive praise. The structure of these descriptive hymns of praise is quite simple.[3]
1. A call to praise God.
2. Reasons for praising God.

This pattern may be partially or fully repeated in this simple formula. Psalm 100 is a well known hymn which follows this pattern. It begins with a call to praise God in 100:1,2: "Make a joyful noise unto the Lord, all ye lands. Serve the Lord with gladness; come before his presence with singing." This is followed with a reason for praising God in 100:3, "Know ye that the Lord he is God; it is he that hath made us, and not we ourselves; we are his people, and the sheep of his pasture." This pattern is repeated with another call to praise God in 100:4, "Enter into his gates with thanksgiving, and into his courts with praise; be thankful unto him, and bless his name," and a second reason for praising God in 100:5, "For the Lord is good; his mercy is everlasting; and his truth endureth to all generations." Although the pattern is fairly simple, this brief psalm of praise contains a great deal of theology. The worshiper is recognizing the importance of coming to God's house to worship and praise God. This is not just a habit, the respectable thing to do, or an issue of obeying parents. Believers understand why God is praised, they have experienced His grace, their hearts are full of motivation for thanksgiving. God created them, God considers them His special people and He provides for their needs. He is good to them, He shows His love again and again, He is faithful in so many ways. He is worthy to be praised.

Sometime these declarative hymns of praise emphasize the call to praise God like Psalm 148:1-5a; 7-13a. It has only two very short sections (5b-6 and 13b-14) which give the reason why God should be praised. Other hymns have very brief calls to praise God (147:1a; 7; 12) but a very long list of reasons for praising Him (147:1b-6; 8-11; 13-20). These hymns fulfill one of the chief purposes for the existence of mankind on earth—the purpose of enjoying and glorifying God.

Since transportation was difficult in those days, people who lived a long way from Jerusalem were able to come to the temple and worship God only a few times each year. No wonder they were thrilled and excited about actually coming to the temple again. When the worshiper joined with the masses to sing the glory of God, it was an inspiring experience. As they sang through the hymn, they would be reminded of the many reasons they had to praise God. God had been good to them (by giving them good crops and plenty of food to eat), God had been faithful to them (by answering a prayer or by fulfilling a promise), God's love was very evident (by giving them good health or by giving them a new child in their family). God's grace was not ignored or taken for granted; it was celebrated to glorify Him and encourage others to put their trust in Him.

Theological significance

1. In times of difficulty believers can bring all their burdens to God, for He always hears and comforts those who come to Him.
2. The prayer for help should not just be centered on the problem or what is needed. It should also focus on God's ability to answer prayer, the believer's commitment to trust God, and the ultimate desire to glorify God for His grace and goodness.
3. God's house is a place of praise and thanksgiving. The joy of the Lord should fill the hearts and lips of those who have been blessed by God.
4. God is to be praised because He is God, we are His people, and He has provided for us.

Notes

1. C. Westermann, *The Psalms: Structure, Content and Message* (Minneapolis: Augsburg, 1980) p. 29-45.
2. Westermann, *The Psalms: Structure, Content and Message*, p. 71-80.
3. Westermann, *The Psalms: Structure, Content and Message*, p. 81-92.

Discussion questions

1. What can we learn about a psalm from its title?
2. What are some similarities and differences between the book of Psalms and our modern hymnbooks?
3. What is the common structure of the lament? How does this structure encourage the people lamenting to overcome the fear and the discouragement of their difficult situation?
4. List some reasons why people praise the Lord in the descriptive hymns of praise in Psalm 33, 111, 135 and 145.
5. Try writing and praying a simple prayer of lament based on a real problem you are facing (following the structure provided above) and also a basic hymn of praise that declares your own reasons for praising God. If you are musical, you might even want to set your hymn of praise to music.

SPECIAL THEMES IN THE PSALMS

2

Psalms 73-150
Time period: 1050-500 B.C.

In addition to the lament and the hymn of praise which were examined in the last chapter, several other types of psalms emphasize special themes and have a unique structure or setting in Israelite life. These include historical psalms, imprecatory psalms, psalms of confession and penitence, wisdom psalms, royal psalms, and messianic psalms. Although these psalms are fewer in number, they contain many important theological ideas and reveal some significant aspects about Israelite worship.

Historical Psalms
Historical psalms are different from other psalms in that they do not relate to a specific event in the life of a believer. Instead they review Israel's history in order to remind the listener of the nation's past sins, to praise God for His gracious deeds on their behalf, or to encourage the people to trust God because He has been faithful in the past.[1]

Psalm 78 is a catalog of God's wondrous deeds which parents taught their children so that the coming generation would have confidence in God, not forget His grace or commandments, and not be rebellious like their fathers (78:5-8). The first section (78:9-20) reviews God's miracles in Egypt, the crossing of the Red Sea, the cloud that led them through the wilderness, the giving of water from the rock, and the Israelites' rebellion when they did not have any water or meat to eat. The second section (78:21-39) records God's anger at the people's unbelief, but also His gracious provision of manna (the bread of angels) and meat from the quails. This paragraph ends by returning to the theme of God's anger at the people's rebellion and unfaithfulness even after He provided for their physical needs. The third section (78:40-53) focuses on how the people in the wilderness forgot God's power displayed in each of the plagues of Egypt. The fourth section (78:54-72) summarizes the nation's entrance into the holy land and defeat of the Canaanites, but also the people's tendency to worship graven images. Because of the people's persistent sinfulness, God abandoned His tabernacle in Shiloh and later rejected the northern tribes of Israel. But God remained faithful to Judah, chose David to be their king and instructed him to build a temple in Jerusalem. Throughout this time God guided the nation and cared for those He loved. This psalm and its themes are similar to other historical psalms (Ps. 105; 106; 135).

Imprecatory Psalms

A number of psalms contain curses or imprecations against the enemies of God's people. Some of these curses are a small part of a lament (Ps. 139:19-22) while other curses take up the major portion of the psalm (Ps. 35; 69; 109). These psalms have caused a certain amount of uneasiness for Christians because they seem to be promoting a vengeful attitude, just the opposite of Jesus' command to love our enemies (Matt. 5:44). Although some believe that these statements are evil, sub-Christian, and a negative part of the old dispensation's ethics, a careful look at these expressions of righteous indignation suggests that they were not motivated by desires for sinful or personal revenge.

The curses in Psalm 109:6-20 reveal that the wicked have lied and made false accusations against the righteous (109:2-5). The believers ask that God would judge these people by taking their lives, leaving their children fatherless, taking their land, cutting off their memory from the earth. This is the way that God Himself said He would righteously reward the wicked for their sinful deeds (109:6-20). Elsewhere, David cries out for God to slay the wicked because they speak against God and they take God's name in vain. David hates those who hate God, he hates them with great hatred (Ps. 139:19-22). But David is not speaking of personal vengeance, for in the very next verse he asks God to search him to see if there is any hurtful or vengeful thought in him (139:23,24). It becomes clear that David is so identifying with God's hatred of sin that he cannot stand it any longer; he wants God to remove it. The modern sense of discomfort with these prayers may be more a commentary on present tendencies to downplay the seriousness of sin. Paul delivered unto death and Satan the man who continued in sin at Corinth (1 Cor. 5) and also cursed anyone who would preach another gospel other than the gospel of Christ (Gal. 1:6-10). Possibly David and Paul were more in tune with God's hatred of sin than many realize. After all, Scripture indicates that God will send some people to hell because of their sins.[2] Both Old and New Testaments encourage believers to love their neighbors (Lev. 19:18; Matt. 19:19), warn against personal vengeance (Deut. 32:35; Heb. 10:30), and teach us to hate and run from sin because God hates it.

Psalms of confession and penitence

A central characteristic of those who love God is their hatred of sin, their desire to turn from sinful attitudes and actions, and their willingness to confess their sin so that they can receive God's forgiveness. Although the Day of Atonement was a national day of humiliation and penitence so that the nation could be cleansed of its sins (Lev. 16), the believers in the Old Testament could acknowledge their sins and receive God's forgiveness at any time. Confessing sins was also closely associated with presenting of the sin offering at the temple. It must be emphasized, however, that the act of offering a sacrifice was not the important element, but the essential thing God was looking for was a broken spirit, the repentant heart of the sinner (Ps. 51:16,17).

Many suggest that the prayers of confession in Psalm 51 and 32 were related to David's sinful sexual relationship with Bathsheba (note the heading of Ps. 51). In Psalm 51 David asks for God's grace and compassion. He wants God to blot out his sins and cleanse him from his iniquities (51:1,2). David acknowledges that sexual relationships outside of marriage are sinful, that he did something that was evil in God's eyes, and that he deserves His judgment (51:3,4). But David is turning from this evil way of life and asking God to purify him, to wash him clean, to create in him a clean heart (51:7-10). He does not want God to forsake him because of his sins; he wants God to restore joy to his life so that he can share what he has learned with others and warn them of his mistakes (51:11-13). Once God has forgiven him (because David has a humble heart, not because he has gone through the ritual of some sacrifice), David will praise God and sing for joy (51:14-17).

Psalm 32 is an illustration of David teaching others about his own experience. At first he tried to hide his sin, to refuse to call it sin, but his conscience weighed heavily upon him during sleepless nights (32:3,4). Finally he confessed his sin and stopped trying to hide his guilt. Then God graciously forgave him (32:4,5) and he enjoyed the blessedness of having his sins removed (32:1,2). Because of this experience, David instructed the people in Israel to pray for forgiveness as soon as they committed a sin (32:6), not to be stubborn like a mule (32:9). Continued sinfulness and an unrepentant attitude bring great sorrow, but confession of sins and trusting in God for forgiveness bring great joy (32:10,11). Certainly David's admonition concerning the importance of confessing sins is in line with the New Testament message that God will be faithful and just and forgive our sins if we will confess them to him (1 John 1:9).

Wisdom Psalms

Although it is a little difficult to identify what a wisdom psalm is, most agree that there are a group of psalms which reflect the teachings of the wisdom books (Ps. 1; 37; 73; 112; 127; 128). Similarities of themes (prosperity or destruction, the righteous or the fool, the suffering of the righteous) and proverbial statements suggest that some of the psalmists had read wisdom writings and believed that their teaching could be used to instruct and encourage Israelite believers.[3]

Psalm 1 contrasts the life of the righteous (1:1-3) and the wicked (1:4,5). The people who are blessed by God do not go to evil people for advice, do not spend their time doing what sinful people do, and they do not mock or scoff at spiritual things. Instead they spend some of their time reading and studying God's Word. Because of this, God prospers what they do (1:1-3). The wicked do not act like the righteous; therefore, they will not stand when God brings His judgment on them (1:4,5). The final comparison contrasts God's care for the righteous with the perishing of the wicked who are without God (1:6).

Psalm 73 is somewhat similar to the book of Job, for both wrestle with the difficult question of why the righteous person suffers, and why so many wicked people seem to prosper (73:3-12). Although it may seem vain to be pure, troubles may embitter us and seem senseless, the psalmist reminds the believer that the end of the wicked will not be happy (73:13-19). In times of trial, people must rest in the promise of God's presence with them (73:23), be assured of receiving their reward at a later time (73:24), get their eyes off their earthly desires, and cling to God for strength (73:25-28).

Royal Psalms

Within this group of psalms are songs about or by an earthly king, as well as songs about the kingship of God. In the first group are Psalms 20, 21, 45, 72, 89, and 132. These psalms call on God to protect his anointed king in Jerusalem and give him victory in his wars against his enemies (Ps. 20). In response to God's deliverance from his enemies, the king is glad, trusts in God, and praises Him (Ps. 21). A song which was probably used at the wedding of one of Israel's kings is recorded in Psalm 45 and psalms about God's covenant with King David (see 2 Sam. 7:1-16) are found in Psalms 89 and 132.

Of equal, if not greater importance, are those psalms which celebrate the kingly rule of God Himself (Ps. 47; 93; 96-99). These are not enthronement psalms which accompanied an autumn festival in which God was made king as some have suggested.[4] In the theocracy established when Israel first became the people of God, it was understood that God was their ruler and king. This is why Gideon refused to become Israel's king (Judg. 8:23). The danger of having an earthly king was the temptation for him to rule instead of allowing God to be the supreme king (1 Sam. 8:4-7; 12:12-15). The great king who is to be feared is God

Himself (Ps. 47:2). He reigns over all the nations of the earth and He is to be praised (47:6,7). He is worshiped because He is king over all gods (95:3; 97:9), because He will judge all nations (96:9-13), and because He rules the earth with strength and justice (99:4). He is holy and an almighty king, therefore we should worship Him as our master, lord, and king of our lives.

Messianic Psalms

There are a number of problems associated with interpreting messianic psalms. Some people are very skeptical of messianic interpretations and deny that these psalms were prophetic of the coming of Jesus. They believe that these passages refer to David or someone who lived in Old Testament times. Others accept the New Testament evidence that these refer to Jesus, but then read into the Old Testament passage information which was never understood until Jesus came. It seems that a middle course between these extremes must be maintained. The interpreter must accept the witness of the New Testament that these refer to Jesus the Messiah, but one should explain these messianic psalms on the basis of what was revealed to David, not what was revealed hundreds of years later when the gospels were written. Since the Davidic psalms say nothing about Jesus' virgin birth (it was revealed about 250 years later in Isa. 7:14), it appears that David did not know about this.

Psalms 2 and 110 are messianic psalms which predict that God will install His anointed son as king in Zion (2:6). This king will rule the whole earth and all people will submit to him or be destroyed (2:8-12). This prophecy refers to the second coming of Christ when He will come in power to rule the earth and set up His kingdom. Psalm 110 reveals that the messianic king, who was David's lord, will one day sit on the right hand of God and rule over the whole earth.

Some commentators disagree on how to understand some psalms which do not appear to be messianic in the Old Testament, but are quoted in the New Testament. Some believe that there is a double fulfillment of these psalms, while others believe that there is a typological fulfillment. In all cases it is important that the student first try to figure out what these passages would have meant to David or other Israelite believers.

Theological significance

1. God is sovereignly involved in directing each believer's life.
2. In spite of human sinfulness, God graciously offers forgiveness to those who will repent.
3. God hates sin and will judge the sinner.
4. God's way of life has been revealed in His Word. The righteous person will wisely avoid sinful ways and follow God's way.

5. God is the king of this world. He reigns with all power and with perfect justice. In the end He will defeat every other power on earth, and all will praise Him.
6. At the end of time God will send the Messiah, who now sits at the right hand of God, to defeat the forces of evil and rule the whole earth.

Notes

1. H. C. Leupold, *Exposition of the Psalms* (Grand Rapids: Baker, 1969), p. 561,562.
2. C. S. Lewis, *Reflections on the Psalms* (1961), p. 31, suggests that the psalmists took right and wrong more seriously. They also knew the difference between the two.
3. W.S. LaSor, D.A. Hubbard, and F.W. Bush, *Old Testament Survey* (Grand Rapids: Eerdmans, 1982), p. 522,23.
4. S. Mowinckel, *The Psalms in Israel's Worship* (Nashville: Abingdon, 1962), strongly supported this theory on the basis of Babylonian rituals. There is no evidence that Israelites had such a ritual, and if they did it would certainly be quite different from the pagan religion in Babylon.

Discussion questions

1. Why is it important to sing and read about God's great acts of grace and judgment in the past?
2. When would it be appropriate to pray an imprecatory prayer? What attitudes must the believer exhibit or avoid when praying such prayers?
3. List some wise sayings that you can apply to your life from Psalms 37, 73, 127, and 128.
4. Try to remember your last prayer of confession and then compare it to David's confession of sin in Psalm 51. Was your prayer as serious as David's prayer about the transformation of your heart? How has the way you think and act changed that would confirm your findings?
5. What are some areas of your life where God is king and ruler? What does Romans 8:14-17 say about the struggle within us for control of our lives. What areas of your life would you like to see controlled by God's power and kingship? How does a person bring about this change?

WISDOM

3

Job and Ecclesiastes

The cultural setting of the wisdom books is probably more important than the historical context in which they were written, for wisdom ideas were not tied to one particular time frame. They deal with life's basic issues (what is wise and foolish, suffering, raising children, the vanity of life without God, the need to fear God) which are faced in every age. Some wisdom writings were constructive (like Proverbs), providing instructions on how a person was to live successfully within the societal structure and within the moral order that God designed. Other wisdom writings raised questions about a person's ability to successfully understand and live within the social and moral order that exists (Ecclesiastes and Job). Both approaches recognized that God rules the world and that a right relationship with Him produces true wisdom.

Wisdom literature was popular in Egypt (Exod. 7:11; 1 Kings 4:30; Isa. 19:11,12), Babylonia (Dan. 1:20; 4:6,7), and Edom (Obad. 8; Job 2:11) so it is not surprising to find a section of the Bible devoted to wisdom.[1] It appears that the wise man Job was from the Edomite city of Uz (1:1). Solomon, Job, and pagan writers had a certain amount of wisdom that came from their natural limited human understanding of life, for God revealed Himself to all people in nature and conscience (Rom. 1-2). Wisdom included the proper understanding of cultural and moral regulations as well as the proper relationship between mankind and the spiritual powers in the world. Of course the wisdom of the pagan gods was not in agreement with or as powerful as God's wisdom (Exod. 7-9; Dan. 2-5; 1 Cor. 1:18-2:16).

Biblical wisdom literature is also unique when compared to the books of Moses or the prophets, for wisdom is not directly related to the covenant relationship with Israel. Instead it deals with the question of God's just and ordered rule of the whole world.

Job
Does God rule the earth with justice?

Although Job had many children and was a wealthy herdsman like some of the patriarchs in Genesis, this kind of lifestyle existed during the time of King David and was still common in the remote areas of the ancient Near East up until the 19th or 20th century A.D. Since wisdom literature in Israel was associated with the life and times of Solomon and Hezekiah (1 Kings 3:3-14; 10:6,7,23-25; Prov 1:1; 25:1; Eccles. 1:1), many believe the book of Job came from that period.[2]

Outline of Job

The author of Job reveals information concerning the unseen spiritual battles that go on in this world. Since some of these events are a mystery to mankind, it is impossible for people to always understand the reason that God allows certain things to happen. This shows that reason cannot be the sole basis of a person's relationship with God. Although wisdom writings encourage a rational understanding of life, they recognize the limitations of human wisdom and call people to fear God and put their faith in Him.

Does Job serve God out of pure motives?

Job was a righteous man who feared God and turned away from all evil (1:1,8; 2:3). But the adversary of God and man thought that Job feared God only because He had blessed him with many children and great wealth, not out of pure motives. After God allowed Satan to test Job by taking his children and possessions, Job remained faithful to God because he believed that the God who freely gives also has the right to take away (1:20-22). In a second trial, God allowed Satan to afflict Job with a terrible skin disease. Still Job did not blame God, even though his wife suggested that he should curse God and die (2:9,10).

Is Job guilty or is God unjust?

Job's three friends came to comfort and restore him. After an initial period of mourning and silence was observed, a pattern of alternating speeches developed. But sometimes the one speaking is not directly answering the charges of the preceding speaker.

The series begins with Job lamenting that he was born and wishing that he were dead (3:1-26).

Eliphaz the Temanite (an Edomite city) responded with three speeches (4-5; 15; 22). In the first he told Job to be strong, for he had encouraged others with similar advice. He must put his confidence in God, for He cares for the innocent and judges the wicked (4:3,6-9). When people fall into sin, they should be happy when God reproves them. This is the way God works to redeem those in sin (5:17-20). This was the basic theological stance taken by Eliphaz and the other two friends throughout their dialogue with Job. Eliphaz mocked Job's windy and unprofitable words (15:1-6) because Job rejected the wisdom of the traditional wise men and claimed to have some secret knowledge from God (15:7-13). Eliphaz knew that God judged the wicked (15:18-35), therefore he reproved Job for claiming that he was innocent (20:1-20). He encouraged him to repent so that God could restore him (22:21-30).

Bildad responded to Job three times (8; 18; 26) with a theological argument similar to that of Eliphaz. But it is clear that he had less sympathy in his voice. God is just and does not pervert justice; if Job would seek Him and repent, God would restore him (8:3-7,20). Job must accept this traditional wisdom, for the wicked who forget God are like a plant with no water (8:8-15), but the righteous are like a plant with water (8:16-20). The fate of the wicked is trouble and eventually death (18:5-21).

Zophar's two speeches (11; 20) were caustic and very unsympathetic to Job's physical and mental trials. He coldly dismissed Job's statement that he was innocent. It sounded like boasting to him (11:3,4). He thought that Job did not understand God's ways. If he would repent, God would restore him (11:7-15). Zophar totally rejected Job's observation that sometimes God does not judge the wicked (20:4-29).

In between these speeches Job lamented the anguish of his painful existence (7:3-8), questioned why God was attacking him (7:11-19), and rejected the advice of his worthless comforters (6:14-27). Job wanted to prove that he was right with God, but it was impossible to take God to court (9:1,2,14-16). How could he prove that God sometimes treats the wicked and the righteous the same way (9:22)? Unfortunately there was no umpire to oversee this case, to decide if Job was just or if God was treating him unjustly (9:33-35). Job loathed his sickness so much (10:1-7), he decided to go ahead with a court case against God (13:1-19).

First Job rejected his friends' traditional wisdom, because all true wisdom and power belong to God (12:1-6,13-25). From that point on his speeches were directed to God. God had shattered his life while he was at peace, attacked him on every side and made Job out to be his enemy (16:7-17). He cried out for a heavenly witness or advocate to notice his plight (16:18-22), for his friends were useless comforters. Surely the righteous will be appalled at the way his friends and God have treated him (17:1-10; 19:1-12). People acted like he was a social outcast, and his family, servants, and peers despised him (19:13-22). His hope was that an eternal record would be kept so that his redeemer might justify him in the end (19:23-27).

The heart of Job's case was that God did not always bless the righteous and judge the wicked as his friends claimed. No, many wicked people were happy and prosperous (21:7-34; 24:1-17). Job wanted God to explain His execution of justice in this lawsuit and to tell Job why he, an innocent man, was suffering. Although God's power and wisdom are often beyond human understanding (26:5-14), Job needed an explanation. He was innocent (27:1-6) but he was judged. He needed something to counter the traditional wisdom viewpoint that God judges only the wicked. This implied that Job must be wicked (27:7-23).

Where can wisdom be found?

The author of Job inserted a short poem about the difficulty of finding wisdom.[3] Although people have found precious stones and metal deep in the earth, where can they find wisdom? It is the most valuable thing but it is hidden from mankind. Indeed, the only true source of wisdom is God.

Job's claim of innocence

The dialogue between Job and his friends ended in frustration for both sides. Job gave one final summary of his arguments to end his case. Formerly he was blessed by God and he was a respected and honored man in society (29:1-25). But now he is mocked and dishonored in society and attacked by God (30:1-31). Yet he is innocent of a whole list of great and small sins (31:1-40). God must explain to him how this can be just.

Elihu's defense of God's justice

Although Elihu was not introduced at the beginning of the dialogue, he now speaks to justify God's action and refute Job's claims. After a long introduction to defend his right to speak (32:6-22), Elihu refuted Job's claim that God never answers people's inquiries. He spoke through visions, through painful diseases, and through a mediator who will deliver those who repent of their sins (33:13-28). By reaffirming the justice of God, Elihu refuted Job's claim that God was not dealing justly by treating everyone the same (34-35). Finally he described various aspects of the world that demonstrate the wonders of God's sovereign rule. Some of these were so beyond human comprehension that it is preposterous for anyone to question anything God does (36-37).

God's power and wisdom are revealed

Finally the Lord answered Job in two speeches. First He challenged Job to teach him about the measurements of the earth. It was God who created and controls the sea, the light, the underworld and the weather through His power and wisdom (38:1-38). He also understands and controls the lion, deer, ox, ostrich, horse, and bird of prey (38:39-39:30). Can Job find some fault in God in all of this? No, he is silent in the presence of God's power and wisdom (40:1-5).

In God's second speech He challenges Job to teach him about justice (40:6-14). But Job does not have the power or the wisdom even to bring the beasts Leviathan and Behemoth to justice, so how can he pretend to teach God who made these beasts (40:15-41:34). In response, Job admitted that he complained to God about things he really did not know about. Now that his eyes are opened to the mystery of God's glorious ways, he is humbled (42:1-5).

Job's restoration

God also revealed that Job's friends were wrong and Job was correct. Job was not suffering for some great evil that he had committed. The three friends confessed their wrong and Job prayed for them. Then God gave Job more children and blessed him with great riches.

Theological significance

1. God may allow people to be tested so that they can demonstrate their dedication to God and His will for their lives.
2. It is an error to conclude that all sickness and trouble come because of sin. Sometimes the innocent suffer and the wicked are not immediately judged.
3. Since people on earth cannot see the whole picture and have a very limited understanding of God's plans and wise purposes, they should not question God's justice.
4. Comforting the sufferer is not achieved by naive accusations, but by identifying with their grief and praying for God's mercy.

In the New Testament James remembered the patience of Job during his long period of suffering and encouraged his readers to wait faithfully for God's compassion.

The mysterious yet wise plan of God which governs the way He rules the world is treated at several points in the New Testament. Jesus told his disciples that a certain blind man was not blind because he or his parents had sinned. He was blind so that God's power could be displayed in Jesus; it was not a punishment for sin (John 9:1-3).

Ecclesiastes
Distinguishing between vanity and the good

The repeated negative statements about the vanity of life under the sun has frequently resulted in a negative attitude toward the value of this book. It appeared to be pessimistic, fatalistic, cynical, and without much spiritual significance. But this view ignored the numerous statements about what is good and enjoyable for mankind. People are to fear God and remember that every good thing that we have is a gift that comes from God. Because of these two emphases (vanity and good), it is best to see the author as a realist who recognized that life was full of frustrating and vain situations. But he also realized that there are some values that give life meaning and he encouraged the reader to be wise by knowing what has value and what is useless.

Outline of Ecclesiastes

Experience reveals much vanity in life	Eccles. 1:1-6:12
Much repetition is vain	1:1-11
Striving only brings vanity	1:12-2:26
No one can fully understand life or God	3:1-4:16
The vanity of hypocrisy and riches	5:1-6:12
Experience shows what is good	7:1-12:7
Things that are good and wise	7:1-29
It is good to enjoy life	8:1-9:9
Work, be wise, avoid foolishness	9:10-10:20
Remember your Creator and fear God	11:1-12:7

The preacher/teacher was a king in Jerusalem who was the son of David (1:1,12). The only one who fits this description was Solomon. Was this a book written about Solomon or did Solomon ever come to his senses and realize the vanity of his ways? Some suggest that he may have repented of his evil ways (1 Kings 11:1-11) when he was about to die, but the Bible never records anything about any revival at the end of his life.

Experience reveals much vanity in life

What advantage do people gain from all their work? People profit about as much as the sun which goes round and round and is never done, about as much as the wind or the water that never finish their work. All this work seems to be in vain.

Constantly striving after wisdom is no answer, for that only increases one's grief (1:12-18). Striving after the pleasures of wine, possessions, more servants, gold, or beautiful music does not give lasting satisfaction (2:1-11). Although it is better to be wise, both the wise and the foolish die and are soon forgotten. Life and all its work sometimes seem futile, for who knows, maybe children will waste it all. The best thing to do is to enjoy whatever God has given. He will give wisdom and joy to the good person, but will take away what little the foolish person has to enjoy (2:24-26).

It is wise to recognize that there is a proper time for every experience of life: war and peace, birth and death (3:1-8). God has secretly arranged all these things so that people will fear Him. Although people cannot fully understand God's plan, they should rejoice, work hard, and see life as God's gift of grace (3:9-15). Life may seem unjust at times, but people are not much better at judging this than the beasts. God will judge every person's deeds, particularly those who oppress, are selfish, workaholics, over-competitive, or unteachable (4:1-16). These characteristics lead to vanity, not wisdom.

It is vain to come hypocritically to the temple to worship God and say things that one does not really mean, for God knows what everyone is doing. All that God requires is that one fear Him (5:1-7). Dependence on riches is also futile, for it will not satisfy and cannot be taken after death (5:10-6:9). It is best to just enjoy the things that God has given. These are gifts from God, and He can give people the ability to be content with what they have (5:18-6:2).

Experience shows what is good

Using some deep proverbs, Ecclesiastes suggests that it is good to think about the shortness of life, to listen to the wise person, to be patient, not to yearn for the good old days, and to be content with one's lot (7:1-14). Although it is hard to understand why the righteous sometimes suffer, the wise person will fear God and escape trouble by avoiding extremes. Wisdom gives a person some strength against the sinful ways that have affected everyone (7:19,20). Unfortunately there are very few wise people around, even though God originally made everyone righteous. One simple way to demonstrate wisdom is to be loyal and obedient to the laws and political rulers (8:1-9), though it is clear that governments do not always reward the deeds of the righteous (8:10-14). Although people may not understand why God allows these things, they can rest assured that every life is in God's hands (8:16-9:1). One day everyone will die, but before that day it is important that people be happy and enjoy life with their family, work hard at their responsibilities, and see wisdom as a great resource for a good life (9:2-18). This will help each person avoid foolish actions, like falling in the pit that was dug to trap someone else (10:1-20).

People need to live by faith (11:1-6), rejoice, and think about God the creator before old age sets in and they die (12:1-7). There is much vanity in life, so those who fear God and obey His commandments will learn wisdom from the people that God, the Good Shepherd, has put in their lives (12:8-14).

Theological significance

1. People who are always striving after more wisdom, pleasure, or wealth will find futility, not true satisfaction.
2. Although people cannot fully understand God's plans, He is in control of all the aspects of each person's life.
3. People should enjoy the food, family, and work that God has given them—these are God's gifts.
4. Above all things, fear God and obey His commandments, be wise and walk circumspectly in this evil world.

Notes

1. *The Ancient Near East*, ed. J. Pritchard (Princeton: Princeton University Press, 1969) includes a series of wisdom texts that archeologists have found in Egypt and Babylonia. It is interesting to note that they treat some of the same basic concerns that are found in the Bible, but solutions were sometimes quite different.
2. J. E. Hartley, "Job," *International Standard Bible Encyclopedia*. Vol. II (Grand Rapids: Eerdmans, 1982), p. 1065,1066.
3. It is not very clear who is speaking this beautiful poem in chapter 28. It hardly seems consistent with Job's speeches. Note that the next chapter introduces Job, implying that he was not speaking in ch. 28. F. I. Anderson, *Job* (Downers Grove: InterVarsity Press, 1976), concludes it was written by the author/editor of the book.

Discussion questions

1. Why do people suffer? Give several suggestions from Job.
2. If you were one of Job's comforters and did not know about Job 1-3, what would you have said to Job?
3. What did Job learn when God spoke to him in 38-41? See 40:1-5 and 42:1-6.
4. Why does the book of Ecclesiastes think that so many things are like striving after wind?
5. Compare Ecclesiastes 2:24-26; 3:12-14; 5:18-20; 9:7-10 to Paul's admonitions in Philippians 4:11-13; 1 Timothy 6:6-11; Hebrews 13:5-6.

INSTRUCTIONAL WISDOM

4

Proverbs and Song of Solomon

The titles of these two books are related to the period of Solomon, the son of David, who was king in Jerusalem about 970-930 B.C. (Prov. 1:1; 10:1; 25:1; Song of Sol. 1:1; 3:7,9,11; 8:11,12). When Solomon became king he asked God for wisdom so that he could lead the nation and accurately judge between what was right and wrong (1 Kings 3:6-12). God gave him a wise and discerning heart; more wisdom than anyone before him and anyone who would be born after him. The Queen of Sheba testified to his wisdom (1 Kings 10:1-8) and, according to 1 Kings 4:32, Solomon spoke 3000 proverbs and wrote 1005 songs. This means that the entire content of Proverbs and the Song of Solomon is only a small percentage of his total writings. No one knows what the book looked like at the end of Solomon's life, but Proverbs 25:1 indicates that some of these sayings were not collected into the book of Proverbs until the time of Hezekiah. The introductions to chapters 30 and 31 reveal that sayings from Agur and King Lemuel were included within this collection. The date and historical background of these men are unknown but many would place them after the time of Hezekiah.

The Song of Solomon contains a series of songs which are also very difficult to date. These songs may have some distant connection with the wedding songs used by Arabs hundreds of years later in Syria, but this evidence relates more to the cultural background rather than the date of the book. A better comparison might be the wedding song in Psalm 45. Since no direct evidence indicates that the songs in the Song of Solomon were originally sung at a wedding (the material after 5:1 took place after the wedding), it is wiser to simply view these songs as love poems and not assume that they were used at a wedding.[1] Some believe these songs were written about Solomon's wedding with his Shulammite bride, but not by Solomon himself.

Over the years, there has been considerable debate over the meaning of this song. Many believe that it is an allegory of God's love for Israel and/or for the church. To others it is simply a literal story about married love. Actually, it is both—a historical story with two themes of meaning. In one theme we learn about love, marriage, and sex; and the other theme demonstrates God's overwhelming love for His people.

Archeologists have found brief songs and proverbial statements among the writings of the Sumerians, Babylonians, and Egyptians.[2] Although songs and proverbial sayings were common among the uneducated, the upper class ideas discussed in these collections of proverbs suggest that they were used in the process of educating young men who would serve in the king's royal court (Prov. 14:35; 22:29; 23:1,20). Of course, those who knew these proverbs probably taught these principles to people outside the court.

Proverbs

The wisdom contained in the book of Proverbs is arranged in a variety of stylistic formulas — a) antithetical statements which contrast opposites: "The thoughts of the righteous are right; but the counsels of the wicked are deceit" (Prov. 12:5); b) comparisons which frequently draw on nature: "As cold waters to a thirsty soul, so is good news from a far country" (Prov. 25:25); c) "better" comparisons that rank certain kinds of behavior as preferable: "It is better to dwell in the wilderness, than with a contentious and an angry woman" (Prov. 21:19); d) numerical sayings: "There be three things which are too wonderful for me, yea, four which I know not" (Prov. 30:18); e) admonitions concerning wise behavior: "Bow down thine ear, and hear the words of the wise, and apply thine heart unto my knowledge" (Prov. 22:17); f) prohibitions which warn against foolish behavior: "Labour not to be rich; cease from thine own wisdom" (Prov. 23:4).

Although parts of the book of Proverbs are not as cohesively held together as some other sections, there are several units that can be identified.

Outline of Proverbs

Proverbs do not give absolute laws concerning what will happen, nor do they prophesy the outcome of certain behaviors. Proverbs draw on the experience of many people in order to instruct younger people on how this world works. Certain character traits and actions bring good results and God's blessing, so a person would be wise to follow these. Other character traits and behavior patterns bring trouble and failure, so the wise person will avoid these in order that their relationships with God and with other people will be just and righteous.

The purpose of proverbs

The purpose of these proverbs was to give the reader wisdom, knowledge, understanding, wise behavior, justice, honesty, prudence, and discretion. The person who wishes to be known for these characteristics will want to study this book often.

Instructions to be wise

Wisdom is avoiding sinful companions (1:8-19), untrue speech (4:20-27), sexual immorality (5:1-23; 6:20-35; 7:1-27), laziness (6:6-11). and deceit (6:12-15). Instead people should fear God (1:7; 2:5; 3:7; 9:10), seek after the wisdom that God gives (2:6), trust in God with all their hearts (3:5), accept God's discipline (3:11,12), honor God with their wealth (3:9), be just and honest toward other people (2:7,8), and freely give to those in need (3:27,28). God created this world through His wisdom (3:19), put the mountains where they are, established the stars and planets in the heavens, set the boundaries for the oceans and rejoiced over what He did (9:22-31). He knows how the world works and is sovereignly in control of it, so the wise person will fear Him and accept His guidelines for life.

The proverbs of Solomon

Although this section includes fewer topical groupings of verses, various themes are emphasized again and again in these antithetical sayings. God's sovereign control over the affairs of mankind is certain because He cares for the righteous when they are in trouble (10:3), He gives blessings and riches (10:6,22), and lengthens a person's life (10:27). God's eyes see everything that people do (15:3), He even knows their motives (16:2; 17:3; 21:2), therefore He will destroy the house of the proud (15:25). Although people make plans for the future, it is God who answers their prayers and directs their steps according to His own purposes (16:1,4,9,33; 19:21). Victory in war comes from God (21:31) and He will repay those who do evil (20:22).

The wise person will not act like the fool, will avoid wickedness, slander, laziness, pride, deception, cruelty, and anger; but will fear God and walk in His ways so that life will be long and blessed (14:2,26,27; 15:16,33; 16:6; 19:23; 22:4). True wisdom brings people into a right theological relationship with God and a right social relationship with other people.

Admonitions and warnings

This section, which has many similarities with the Egyptian *Admonitions of Amenemope*, is more like a series of laws, rather than proverbs. Many paragraphs begin: "Do not..." and they give a warning not to oppress the poor (22:22), not to associate with hot-tempered people (22:24), not to concentrate on becoming rich (23:4), not to withhold discipline from a child (23:13), not to envy the life of the sinner (23:17; 24:1,19), nor rejoice when the wicked fall (24:17). In most cases a reason is given to explain why such action is unwise (22:23—"For the Lord will plead their cause;" 24:18—"Lest the Lord see it and it displeases him").

The wise person will trust in God (22:19), desire to follow the way of wisdom (24:3-7), respect those who have authority (24:21), show no partiality in judgment (24:23), and work hard (24:30-34).

Hezekiah's collection of proverbs)

The diverse proverbs collected by Hezekiah in this section are particularly well developed. "A word fitly spoken is like apples of gold in pictures of silver" (25:11). "If thine enemy be hungry, give him bread to eat;...For thou shalt heap coals of fire upon his head" (25:21,22). "Answer a fool according to his folly, lest he be wise in his own conceit" (26:5). "As a dog returneth to his vomit, so a fool returneth to his folly" (26:11). These and many other rich comparisons provide a gold mine of practical advice for any person who truly wishes to be as wise as Solomon. Those who have eyes should read and be opened to the light.

The words of Agur and Lemuel

The wise man Agur admits that he does not understand everything that God does (30:2-4) but he desires that God would teach him wisdom and keep him from deception (30:8-9). He then gives a series of numerical wisdom sayings related to the amazing behavior of people and animals (30:10-33). King Lemuel warns against the evils of drinking too much wine (31:1-9).

The virtuous wife

The last paragraph is an acrostic poem describing the virtue, diligence, skill, wisdom, piety, generosity, and inner beauty of a woman who is wise and fears the Lord. She is an excellent woman and a wonderful gift from God.

Theological significance

1. Fearing God is the first step to gaining wisdom.
2. God created this world and runs it according to His wise principles.

3. Foolish people reject God and His ways, but the wise trust Him and will enjoy His blessing.
4. God has set down guidelines to govern righteous interpersonal relationships between people. A wise person will learn them and follow them.

Song of Solomon

This book is like no other in the Old Testament. It is not a sermon like the prophetic texts, but a series of dialogues between a man and a woman, a chorus of the daughters of Jerusalem and a woman, and dialogues within dreams. Since Israel, the covenant, and God's activity with mankind are not key issues within these discussions, there were some early Jewish debates concerning its inclusion within the canon of Scripture. Others were offended by its focus on what appears to be almost a lustful concentration on the beauty of the human body. Consequently "more sanctified" interpretations were developed which saw this imagery as symbolical of the love between God and Israel, or for Christians, the love between Christ and the church. This led to exaggerated allegorical interpretations which were not connected to the historical or grammatical meaning of the text.

While most find only two main characters in this love story, some believe there is a love triangle within the book. Solomon was trying to woo a beautiful country girl, but she was in love with a plain shepherd boy from the country. The drama describes the tension that developed because of these conflicting loyalties.[3] Since the presence of the shepherd boy is not explicit in this story, this interpretation is not preferred.

In light of the important place that love has in the relationships between a man and a woman, it should not be too surprising to find a biblical discussion of this topic. Elsewhere Scripture condemns the perverse sexual relationships of the people of Sodom and Gomorrah (Gen. 19), has a long series of laws about purity and sexuality (Lev. 15; 18; 20), condemns David for his sin with Bathsheba (2 Sam. 11-12), abhors the prostitution that went on at Baal temples (1 Kings 14:24; 2 Kings 23:7), and warns young men to stay away from evil women (Prov. 7). In these songs there is a positive description of love and sexuality.

Outline of Song of Solomon

Mutual expressions of love	Song of Sol. 1:1-2:7
The two meet in the country	2:8-3:5
The wedding procession and marriage	3:6-5:1
The bride longs for her lover	5:2-6:9
Bridegroom's assurances of love	6:1-8:4
Final affirmations of love	8:5-14

A brief description of the events within each of these episodes will help clarify the movement of the action and the emphasis on expressing love for the one that is loved.

Mutual expressions of love

The woman desires to be with the king in his chambers (1:2,3), but in all humility she does not see herself as beautiful (1:5-7). Solomon tells her how beautiful she is (1:9-10,15); then she thinks about (1:12-14) and speaks about her admiration of Solomon and his house (1:16,17). She still thinks she is just an average girl, like a common lily (2:1), but the great Solomon has caused her to be lovesick (2:3-6).

The two meet in the country

One day Solomon went to this young lady's country village and found her (1:8,9). It is spring and he calls her to come and spend some time with him (2:10-14). When he is gone she dreams about him, she goes looking for him at night, and finally finds her love (3:1-5). She cannot stand to be without him.

The wedding procession and marriage

A grand picture of the wedding procession with soldiers and the king carried on a couch begins the preparations for the wedding day (3:6-11). Solomon praises his bride's outward appearance (4:1-6) and desires to go away with her to explore her love and the sexual pleasures of her garden (4:7-15). She accepts his love and he enters her garden of love (4:16-5:1).

The bride longs for her lover

After the wedding the bride misses her absent husband. In her dreams the lovers are living on different schedules and are separated from one another (5:2-7). She is desperate to find him but he is gone. All she can do is sing a song of praise which expresses her deep love for her husband (5:10-16). Finally he returns to her garden of love (6:2,3) and tells of his love for her (6:4-9).

The bridegroom's assurances of love

Solomon reassures his bride of her beauty and his deep love for her (7:1-10). She desires to take him away into the country (and away from business), maybe back to her home, so that they can better enjoy their love for one another (7:11-8:3).

Final affirmations of love

The couple go away and love is awakened near her home (8:5,6). She describes the strength of the power of love and how precious it is (8:6,7). Although she used to be a young immature girl who was pure and did not know a man (8:8,9), she has now found Solomon and willingly gives herself to him (8:10-12).

Theological significance

1. Love expresses appreciation for the beauty (physical and mental) of the one loved and results in a powerful commitment of devotion and mutual fulfillment.
2. Love can be given, but not required or purchased.
3. Sexual purity before marriage is essential, otherwise it will not strengthen the unique bond of love within marriage.

Notes

1. G. L. Carr, *The Song of Solomon* (Downers Grove: InterVarsity, 1984), p. 26-32, discusses various approaches to interpreting the Song of Solomon.
2. G. L. Carr, "The Love Poetry Genre in the Old Testament and the Ancient Near East," *The Journal of the Evangelical Theological Society* 25 (1982), p. 489-98.
3. F. Delitzsch, *Commentary on the Song of Songs and Ecclesiastes* (London: T. & T. Clark, 1985).

Discussion questions

1. What do Proverbs 2-7 have to say about sexual behavior outside of the marriage relationship?
2. Using a concordance, look up the references in Proverbs for one of the following words: lazy/laziness; tongue; discipline; fear. List the references and then write a brief paragraph about this topic that you can share with someone else.
3. If people fear God, how does this effect their practical day-to-day life?
4. How would you define love? What are some characteristics of love in the Song of Solomon?
5. How can human love between two people help us understand something of God's love for us? What should characterize our love for Him?
6. What are the various interpretations of Solomon's song?

UNDERSTANDING AND INTERPRETING THE PROPHETS

5

Scripture Reading: Deuteronomy 13:1-5; 18:14-22;
1 Kings 18:16-46; Jeremiah 23:9-40; Ezekiel 1:22-3:21;
Micah 3:5-8

Diversity among the prophets

When most people speak of the prophets, they immediately think of individuals like Isaiah or Daniel because they wrote some of the most important prophetic books of the Bible. There is no doubt that these were two key individuals that God used to proclaim His word, but there were many other men and women in Israel who had the ability to speak prophetically, but did not write books (the names of some of them are even unknown).

Because Moses had so much trouble with the people of Israel during their wilderness journeys, God encouraged him to share the burden with the seventy elders of Israel (Num. 11:10-17). After the seventy elders of Israel consecrated themselves to the Lord, God sent His Spirit upon them and they prophesied. Since these men prophesied only this one time, they were not considered official prophets (11:24-25).

Some prophets like Samuel, Jeremiah, and Ezekiel were also priests, thus they filled two different functions in Israelite society. A few Levitical priests prophesied as they sang praise to God and played musical instruments in the temple (1 Chron. 25:1-5). Other prophets like Gad and Nathan (who were sometimes called seers) had no official role in the temple but delivered God's word from time to time and functioned as moral and political advisors to King David (2 Sam. 12:1-15; 24:11; 1 Chron. 21:9). A few prophets like Elisha did miracles (2 Kings 4) but most did not have these powers. Some prophets worshiped together as a group or band of prophets at the time of Samuel (1 Sam. 10:5). Later the sons of the prophets who were in Bethel and Jericho at the time of Elisha lived and studied together (2 Kings 2:1-18). Most later writing prophets worked by themselves and made no reference to other prophets around them.

Miriam was the first woman to be a prophetess and a singer of God's praise (Exod. 15:20), Deborah was a prophetess and judge over Israel (Judg. 4:4), and Huldah was the prophetess who served Josiah and identified the book found in the temple as the law of Moses (2 Kings 22:14-20).

These examples show that God used very different people from varied backgrounds to proclaim His words in many different contexts. This diversity was needed in order to allow God's word to affect all aspects of Israelite society. But this diversity also caused some problems, for it became very difficult for some people to distinguish true prophets from false prophets.[1]

Unity among the prophets

The key factor which identified prophets was not their role or parental background, or whether they wrote a prophetic book or not. The main issue was: did God fill these people with His Spirit and speak through them?

The Hebrew word *prophet* means to be God's spokesman, while words for *seer* refer to those who have insight into God's will. Although Baal prophets and other pagan diviners claimed to deliver the will of their gods (Jer. 23:13-22), they spoke out of their own imagination and did not report what was decided in the council of God. The true prophets gave prophecies that were later fulfilled (Deut. 18:20-22), they were known for their moral character and hatred of sin (Mic. 3:8), they worshiped only the God of Israel (Deut. 13:1-5), and they were inspired with courage to declare God's message by the presence of the Holy Spirit within them (Mic. 3:8).

The reception of the message by the prophets

The prophets were messengers of God, delivering His words of judgment as well as His words of encouragement and hope. The method of receiving the divine message has always been partially hidden in mystery. Some prophets describe their "call" to the prophetic office when they saw a vision of God and had the Spirit indwell them (Isa. 6; Ezek. 1-3), but most prophets never had any spectacular call experience. The essential requirement for a prophet was the presence of God's Spirit and the reception of God's words. Through the Spirit's work in the minds and hearts of the prophets, they heard words and saw visions or dreams. The truth that was received was molded and expressed in terms of the language and culture of that day and proclaimed to the people. The prophets' knowledge of Scripture, their cultural habits, and their personal styles of speech influenced how the words were said, but these did not change or corrupt the message. God revealed Himself to the prophets in ways they could understand so that they could communicate His truth in ways that made sense to the average Israelite.

The delivery of the prophetic message

Sometimes the prophets spoke their messages orally but at other times they acted out a dramatic message because the stubborn people of Israel would no longer listen to what they said (Ezek. 4-5). Sometimes their original message was immediately written down on a tablet (Isa. 8:1; Hab. 2:2) but frequently their messages were not collected and written down on a scroll until some time later. Jeremiah 36:2 indicates that Jeremiah's messages from 627 to 605 B.C. were not written down until Baruch recorded them in 605 B.C. Many of the prophets chose to arrange their message in chronological order but others (Jeremiah and Daniel) chose to arrange parts of their book topically.

To make sure that the people of Israel understood that they were speaking for God, the prophets repeatedly began or ended their messages with phrases like "Thus says the Lord; declares the Lord; an oracle of the Lord; the Lord God came unto me and said." These statements assured the people that they were not speaking their own words, but the words of God. They revealed the authority behind the prophets' words and encouraged the listener to take seriously what was said.

The prophets Amos and Hosea delivered God's word to the northern nation of Israel, Jonah gave a message of God's judgment to the foreign nation of Assyria, and Daniel witnessed to Babylonian and Persian kings, but most of the writing prophets preached to the people of Judah. In almost every case God's deep and undeserved grace was evident. He not only warned these nations of His coming judgment but called them to repent of their sins so that they might escape His judgment (even the pagan nations that were Israel's enemies were warned to repent).

The message of the prophets

Since the prophets lived in different countries and delivered their messages over several hundred years, there is quite a variety of topics discussed. Political, social, and religious situations varied, so new messages that fit the needs of each audience were given. Amos emphasized the social injustice in Israel while Hosea focused primarily on God's hatred of Israel's worship of Baal. Obadiah condemned the Edomites for their pride and mistreatment of the Jews when the city of Jerusalem was destroyed, while Habakkuk questioned why God was allowing the wicked to prosper in Jerusalem and why He would use the wicked Babylonians to judge a more righteous nation. Each prophet was unique, but each had a message from God to deliver to a specific audience.

Their messages did have a common understanding of God and His character. The prophets consistently called all people to worship only the God of Israel. They repeatedly condemned sin and encouraged repentance. Their messages frequently reminded the Israelites of God's grace to His people when He brought them up from Egypt (Amos 2:9-11; 3:1,2; 9:7), His deep love for them in making a covenant with them at Mt. Sinai (Jer. 11:1-13), and His demand that they should worship only Him (Jer. 10:1-16). If the people would acknowledge their sin, confess it to God, and turn away from their evil ways, God would bless them (Jer. 3:12-14; 4:1-4). If the people would not respond to God's grace and warning, the covenant curses would fall on the nation (Deut. 27-28) and they would be destroyed.

Although the prophets delivered many messages of doom and destruction, they also saw a future day of peace, righteousness, and blessing that was coming. God would forgive their sins and create a new heart in mankind (Ezek. 34:25-31) through the death of His servant (Isa. 53). He would give them a new covenant (Jer. 31:31-34), His Spirit would powerfully transform them (Joel 2:28,29), and the land would produce abundantly (Amos 9:13-15). The righteous seed of David, the eternal king of Israel, would reign as king in Jerusalem (Isa. 9:1-7; Jer. 23:5-7). The evil nations of the earth will be judged and God's dominion will be established as authority is given to the heavenly Son of Man (Dan. 7:9-14). Then the nations will come to Jerusalem to hear God teach His law and war will end forever (Isa. 2:1-4). A new heaven and earth will come into existence (Isa. 65:17) and the departed spirits of the dead will come to life (Isa. 25:8; Dan. 12:1,2).[2]

Through these messages the prophets hoped to persuade the people of Israel and Judah to turn from their selfish ways and dedicate their lives to God's service. Although the pagan people in Nineveh responded to Jonah's message and the post-exilic community responded to Haggai and Zechariah's challenge to rebuild the temple in Jerusalem, most prophets never record any kind of positive response. These people were without excuse because they heard the word of truth, but in their depraved state they refused to submit to the will of God.

The interpretation of prophecy

Frequently different interpretations of prophetic texts are found in commentaries and theology books because the meaning of some verses is not clearly spelled out. Some of the problems relate to the language of these books. The poetic nature of many prophecies and the use of symbolic language make interpretation difficult. Interpretation problems can also arise because the reader is not aware of the historical situation surrounding the prophet's message. Finally, differences of opinion exist because people come to the text presupposing different theological assumptions, particularly as it relates to the eschatological fulfillment of prophecy related to the Messiah and the establishment of God's kingdom.

Sound principles of interpretation are needed in order to guard against false doctrine or being led astray by wild speculation. The primary goal is to understand what God communicated through each prophet. This is accomplished through historical and grammatical research into the meaning of the text. In-depth research will require knowledge of the Hebrew language and extensive understanding of Israel's history. Fortunately, many good translations of the Hebrew Bible and many commentaries, study Bibles, and concordances are now available to help the average person clarify difficult passages.[3]

When studying each of the prophetic books, begin by reading through the whole book at once (this probably will not be possible for some of the longer books). This will provide a basic understanding of the thrust of the whole book and prevent wrong conclusions based on an incomplete knowledge of what was said. From this reading, and with the help of study resources, a general understanding of the historical background should begin to emerge. Was the prophet preaching in Israel or Judah? Who was the king at this time (usually this is given in the first verses of each book)? What were the prevailing political, social, and religious conditions during this period?

Next, divide the book into topical sections in order to get an outline of the prophet's messages. What were the problems that the prophet was preaching about? Trace the argument of the prophet as he attempts to convince people to accept God's word and act upon it. How do these shorter messages fit together to make up the whole book? Which messages relate to the present situation of the people to whom the prophet delivered his message and which refer to things that will happen in the future?

Now study individual passages in more detail. The difficult poetry or symbolism in a verse can be compared in two different translations, or the meaning of a word can be examined by using a concordance to do a word study. Words that symbolize ideas that are foreign to our culture are especially difficult. For example, *shepherd* is a symbol of kingship (2 Sam. 5:2; Ezek. 34), *cows of Bashan* refer to the rich women of Samaria who are "bossy" and extremely rich (Amos 4:1,2), and *singing hills* are a picture of joy (Isa. 44:23).

Some of the most difficult passages are those which prophesy future events. Ahijah's prophecy to Jeroboam, which was accompanied by the tearing of a garment into twelve pieces (1 Kings 11:29-32), was literally fulfilled a short time later when the twelve tribes of the nation of Israel were divided into two nations (1 Kings 12:15-20). The prophet Ahijah knew what would happen but he did not give any of the details of the situation and he did not give the exact date. In a similar manner, Isaiah told Hezekiah that God would deliver him from the Assyrian king Sennacherib (1 Kings 19:20-34) but he did not say when this would happen or how it would happen. Like these examples, most prophecies do not give all the details of exactly what will happen and do not give the date when God will accomplish what He has promised. The person of faith needs to know what God will do, but faith always involves trusting in Him for many things that are unseen and unknown.

When messianic prophecies are found, the interpreter needs to be careful not to read New Testament fulfillment back into the Old Testament. Although the prophet Isaiah knew that the Messiah would be born of a virgin (Isa. 7:14), he did not know where He would be born or how this would happen. God revealed to Micah that the Messiah would be born in Bethlehem (Mic. 5:2), but never said anything about the census that would bring Mary and Joseph from Nazareth to Bethlehem.

Even more problematic are attempts to fit Old Testament passages into the tribulation and millennial texts of the New Testament. Since God never said anything to any of the Old Testament prophets about the difference between heaven and the millennium (it is only mentioned in Revelation 20), it is very difficult to know whether a prophetic text is referring to a heavenly time period when the new heaven and the new earth will exist or when it is referring to what the book of Revelation calls the millennium. Since what would happen was far more important than when it would happen, the believers had to trust God to fulfill His word. Jesus said that we and the angels do not need to know the dates that God has set (Acts 1:7; Matt. 24:36). Nevertheless, Scripture is not totally without a chronological ordering of events, for a careful comparative study of prophecy shows that the Messiah's tribulation would come before His glorification (Isa. 53) and a similar pattern exists at the end of time.

These prophecies are a source of hope for the future and a warning to be ready for the day of the Lord. They encourage believers to trust in God's sovereign plan for this world in spite of the evil, war, persecution, and natural disasters that will become worse and worse in the future. Old Testament prophecies give basic information about what God will do in the future, but for a fuller and more complete revelation on these topics believers should also read Jesus' words in Matthew 24, Paul's words in 2 Thessalonians 2, and John's words in the book of Revelation. Although many of "the words are closed up and sealed till the time of the end....Blessed is he that waiteth..." (Dan. 12:9,12).

Theological significance
1. God revealed His will to the prophets through the gift of His Holy Spirit.
2. God's message was faithfully communicated by the prophets in words that were meaningful and applicable to those who heard.

3. God progressively (not all at once) revealed information about the future.
4. God's future plans are sure but the date when they will come to pass is known only to Him.
5. God's kingdom will be established; therefore, the believer has hope and looks forward to worshiping at the throne of God.

Notes

1. Gary V. Smith, "Prophecy, False," *International Standard Bible Encyclopedia Vol. III* (Grand Rapids: Eerdmans, 1986), p. 984-86.
2. Smith, "Prophet, Prophecy," *International Standard Bible Encyclopedia Vol. III* (Grand Rapids: Eerdmans, 1986), p. 997-1001.
3. Two texts which give many helpful guidelines for those wishing to develop good interpretive skills are: W. C. Kaiser, *Toward an Exegetical Theology* (Grand Rapids: Baker, 1981) or H. A. Virkler, *Hermeneutics: Principle and Processes of Biblical Interpretation* (Grand Rapids: Baker, 1981).

Discussion questions

1. What are some of the advantages and disadvantages of having so much diversity among the prophets? How does diversity among believers today help spread God's word?
2. What was the basic prophetic understanding of: a) God; b) sin; c) repentance; d) judgment? How much do these differ from the New Testament understanding of these issues?
3. List some reasons why people differ in their understanding of prophecy. Write your interpretation of Isaiah 4:2 and then compare it with another person's interpretation in order to discover why you came to different conclusions.
4. What books do you have that help you discover the historical and grammatical meaning of a verse? What books might give you more information?
5. What regular step-by-step method do you use when studying a book of the Bible? Which steps are the easiest and which are the most difficult?

EARLY PROPHETS FROM ISRAEL

6

Jonah, Amos, Hosea
Time of Ministry: Jonah 790-80 B.C.; Amos 765-60 B.C.; Hosea 755-25 B.C.

Shortly after the death of Solomon (931 B.C., see 1 Kings 11-12), the powerful kingdom which David had established was split into the two nations of Israel (the ten northern tribes) and Judah (the two southern tribes). Jeroboam I, the new king of the northern nation of Israel, set up his own government and army, built a new temple at Bethel (near the southern border) and at Dan (near the northern border), and put non-Levitical priests in charge of the false worship of the two golden calves in these temples. These idols were supposed to represent the God who brought them up from the land of Egypt (1 Kings 12:25-33), but the calves were soon confused with the Canaanite god Baal, the god of fertility and rain, who was also pictured as a bull calf. Before long the Israelites were fully involved with the pagan cult of Baalism. Although God raised up the prophets Elijah and Elisha to defeat and destroy this Baal religion during the time of Ahab and Jezebel (1 Kings 16:29-18:46; 2 Kings 1), it was still deceiving the people of Israel years later when Amos and Hosea were preaching in Israel.

Because of the northern nation's sinfulness, God was angry with them and sent the Syrian kings Hazael and Ben-Hadad to defeat them (2 Kings 13:2-3). In the midst of this oppression, the Israelites cried out to God for mercy. As Jonah prophesied, God had compassion on them and sent the Assyrians to defeat the Syrians (2 Kings 13:4,22,23; 14:25). With this enemy defeated, Israel was able to become powerful and quite prosperous under the leadership of Jeroboam II (793-753 B.C.). Amos, who prophesied during this prosperous period, saw this wealth as the source of a false sense of security (6:1-7), and condemned those who added to their riches by oppressing the poor (Amos 2:6-8; 3:10; 5:10-12). Hosea's ministry continued after Jeroboam's reign, when a series of weak kings ruled Israel with tyranny and assassinations (2 Kings 15). This allowed the strong Assyrian king Tiglath-pileser III to make Israel his vassal (2 Kings 15:19,29; 16:9). The northern nation of Israel was finally taken into Assyrian captivity in 722/721 B.C., a few years after Hosea's prophecy.

Jonah
The great compassion of God

The prophet Jonah had two prophetic messages to deliver to two different nations: Israel and Assyria. Scripture says very little about his prophecies concerning Israel and does not record his exact words. Scripture says that he spoke the word of God early in the reign of Jeroboam II to promise military victories for Israel (2 Kings 14:25). Jonah's prophecy was fulfilled during Jeroboam's reign, but the Israelites did not continue to serve God once they were delivered from their enemies.

The book of Jonah describes the prophet's ministry to the Assyrians in Nineveh early in the reign of Jeroboam II.

Outline of Jonah

God's compassion on Jonah	Jonah 1:1-2:10
Jonah rejects God's commission	1:1-16
Jonah turns to God for salvation	1:17-2:10
God's compassion on Nineveh	3:1-4:11
Nineveh turns to God for salvation	3:1-9
Jonah rejects God's mercy on Nineveh	3:10-4:11

This book is unique when compared to other prophetic books, for it contains only one short statement from his preaching (3:4). It shows that the prophets were real people who were not always perfect. They sometimes struggled with the responsibility of telling others about God's hatred of sin. Jonah learned the hard way that God does not want anyone to perish; He wants everyone to know the truth and repent (1 Tim. 2:4; 2 Pet. 3:9).

God's compassion on Jonah

After receiving God's commission to go to the great Assyrian capital of Nineveh, Jonah chose to reject God's calling for his life. Foolishly, Jonah thought he could hide from God (1:3), avoid the problems he might encounter by preaching in the pagan and violent city of Nineveh, and insure God's destruction of the Assyrians by not warning them of God's impending judgment (4:2). After he boarded a ship going to Tarshish, God did not reject Jonah but brought him to the place where he willingly chose to serve God in Nineveh (3:3). After a storm and the casting of lots, Jonah admitted his guilt and accepted the punishment of certain death in the sea. In compassion, God calmed the sea for the pagan sailors (1:15) and sent a large fish to swallow Jonah, rescuing him from death (1:17). Immediately, the pagan sailors feared God and worshiped him while Jonah prayed for God's help in the belly of the fish (2:1,7). Jonah, who did not want God to be compassionate to the undeserving Assyrians in Nineveh, recognized that God's undeserved compassion had been given to him (2:9), thus he obeyed God's second call (3:1).

God's compassion on Nineveh

Jonah boldly proclaimed the message of destruction in the streets of Nineveh (3:4).[1] To Jonah's surprise, the king and people of Nineveh believed God and, in humility, repented of their violent ways and sought God's mercy (3:5-9). God, in his sovereign freedom, had compassion on Nineveh and did not destroy it.

Ironically, Jonah rejected God's redemptive work in Nineveh and became angry with God (4:1-2).[2] Although Jonah selfishly had compassion on the plant that gave him shade in the hot desert outside of the city of Nineveh, he did not want God to be merciful to the people in Nineveh. This shows the depth of God's love and the danger of a shallow human love for unbelievers.

Theological significance

1. This story reveals that God uses believers to carry out His plan to spread the news of God's hatred of sin and His grace to those who repent and turn to Him in faith.
2. Although God's messengers may reject His will, God's plans are not abandoned. Through God's control of events, His servants will experience His discipline in order to bring them to obedience.
3. Since no one can hide from God, each person must faithfully do God's will and share the message that God has given to them.
4. Limiting God's compassion to His covenant people is a great misunderstanding of God's love and will lead to a great misunderstanding of His will for the believer.

Jesus taught from the book of Jonah in Matthew 12:38-41. He compared the three days that Jonah spent in the fish to the three days he would spend in the earth after his death. He also said that the repentant people of Nineveh would condemn the Pharisees who rejected Jesus' message, a message even greater than Jonah's.

Amos
God will destroy Israel

Amos made his living as a fruit grower and a manager of shepherds[3] in the small village of Tekoa about 6 miles south of Bethlehem (1:1). God instructed him to go to the northern nation of Israel and warn them that God would spare His judgment no longer (7:8,14,15). Although Amos had not been trained in the prophetic schools of his day, he courageously withstood the condemnation of the high priest at the temple at Bethel (7:10-17) and the unbelief of his audience. Because God had spoken to him, he knew it was his responsibility to share the message (3:8).

His prophecy was given two years before a major earthquake (ca. 760 B.C.). Uzziah, king in Judah, and Jeroboam II, king of Israel, were at the height of their military power at this time and a rich upper class was ruling the nation through violence and oppression. The people were going through their religious rituals at the temple at Bethel, but their hearts were not turned toward God (4:6-13). Amos announced the unthinkable: God will destroy His own chosen people, the northern nation of Israel.

Outline of Amos

War oracles against the nations	Amos 1:1-2:16
Oracles against six foreign nations	1:3-2:3
Oracles against Judah and Israel	2:4-16
Confirmation of God's judgment on Israel	3:1-6:14
Reasons for God's judgment	3:1-4:13
Laments because of Israel's false hopes	5:1-6:14
Visions and exhortations about the end of Israel	7:1-9:15
Five visions of God's destruction	7:1-9:10
God will bring restoration after judgment	9:11-15

Amos' skill as a preacher is demonstrated in his blunt castigation of those who were getting rich through oppression, his mockery of those who were not truly worshiping God, and his laments for those who were blindly trusting in false promises. His illustrations are those of a country shepherd (2:13—a wagon with grain on it; 3:12—a shepherd rescuing a lamb from a lion; 9:9—a sieve to separate grain); but his knowledge of world history (1:3-2:3) and his biting sarcasm show that he was very knowledgeable about what was really going on in his world.

War oracles against the nations

When troops would go to war, frequently a prophet or priest would be consulted to ask God's blessing and determine if God would give them victory (Judg. 20:18,26-28). Traditionally, these prophecies would reveal that God would destroy their enemies and give them victory. This would give the soldiers confidence to fight. In chapters 1 and 2 Amos' prophecy follows this same pattern (possibly given before a major battle). He describes the terrible inhumanity (killing pregnant women—1:13) that characterized the nations around Israel and assures them that God would destroy these nations because of their sins (1:3-2:3). But instead of ending his prophecy with news of salvation for Israel, Amos surprised his audience by announcing that Israel was worse than the other nations and would be destroyed. The wealthy and powerful in Israel were selling the poor into slavery for small debts and sexually abusing their servants (2:6-8). They forgot that God hates oppression and had delivered them from the slavery of Egypt years ago (2:9,10). None were to become slaves again.

Confirmation of God's judgment on Israel

Most Israelites rejected Amos' prophecy. They were the chosen people of God; they had been redeemed from Egypt; God loved them (3:1,2). But Amos claimed that the privilege of election carried the responsibility of faithful obedience rather than God's automatic blessing. It is only logical: if a lion roars, it is attacking its prey; if a nation sins, it will be judged by God (3:3-7). God's message through Amos was God's roar; He was about to attack Israel, His prey (3:8). What was their sin? Violence, ignoring the difference between right and wrong (3:9,10), oppression of the poor (4:1), and meaningless worship at their temples (4:4,5). In spite of God's chastening, they never turned to God in true repentance (4:4-11); therefore, they must prepare to meet an angry God (4:12). Amos saw the future destruction and laments the destruction of the nation (5:1-3,16,17). If they would only seek God and be just in their relationships with others, they would live (5:4,14,15). Since God hates their worship (5:21), which included false Assyrian gods (5:26)[4], the day of the Lord will be a day of darkness, not salvation (5:18-20). Amos lamented the false sense of security that wealth gave the rich (6:1-7). They will all die.

Visions & exhortations about the end of Israel

Amos received five visions which pictured the coming destruction on Israel. In the first two, Amos pleaded for God's mercy on Israel (7:1-6). Surprisingly, God was compassionate and delayed the judgment, even though the Israelites did not repent. In the final three visions (7:7-9; 8:1-3; 9:1-4) God revealed that He will spare Israel no longer, He will remove the temple at Bethel, and bring an end to the reign of Jeroboam II. No one will be able to escape from His judgment. Although some thought that God's punishment would never touch them (9:10), Amos reveals that every sinner in Israel will die.

Amaziah, the high priest at the temple at Bethel, accused Amos of treason and told him to go earn his living prophesying back home in Judah (7:10-13). Amos refused to accept what Amaziah said because God sent him to speak His word in Israel (7:14-16).

The book ends with a final message about the restoration of the nation long after its judgment (9:11-15). God's promises will be fulfilled. The kingdom of David will exist again. The land will be unbelievably fruitful and filled with Israelites and Gentiles who call on God's name.

Theological significance

1. All people, Jews and Gentiles, will be held accountable for their sins. God hates violence and inhumanity against the weak.
2. Privilege carries responsibility. God's people will be judged if they take His grace for granted and fail to follow Him.
3. If there is no turning to God, no meeting with Him, "worship" is mere ritual, hypocrisy that God hates.
4. Riches and power can bring a false sense of material security and make one feel there is no need to trust God for the future. A false trust in God's promises can give a false sense of spiritual security and cause a person to feel there is no need to repent.
5. When God speaks, His servants cannot be quiet. Warnings of God's judgment must be given, even when opposed.

In Acts 15:16-18, James used the promise of restoration in 9:11-15 to remind the Jewish members of the early church that God wanted the Gentiles to be part of the church. This opened the door for Paul's missionary efforts among the Gentiles.

Hosea
There is no knowledge of God, no love, no truth

Hosea's ministry (755-25 B.C.) began shortly after the time of Amos and continued almost until Israel was taken captive by the Assyrians in 722/21 B.C. Hosea was born in Israel and married Gomer before the end of the prosperous reign of Jeroboam II (1:1-4). In the years that followed he saw anarchy, war, economic weakness (5:8,9; 8:1), and heavy taxation by the Assyrians (2 Kings 15:19,29). Although his ministry ended before the fall of Israel, his prophecies warned of the approaching destruction of the nation.

Outline of Hosea

Adultery in Israel and Hosea's family	Hosea 1:1-3:5
Covenant lawsuit against Israel for adultery	4:1-14:9
There is no knowledge of God	4:1-6:6
There is no steadfast love for God	6:7-11:11
There is no truth in Israel	11:12-14:9

Hosea uses the marriage relationship as an analogy to describe the love relationship between God and His covenant people. This explains God's agony over Israel's unfaithfulness to their covenant relationship. After describing the tragedy of his own marriage (1-3), Hosea reports on God's divorce case against Israel. This covenant lawsuit contains a series of: a) accusations, b) announcements of punishment, and c) offers of hope. The first two are expected parts of a divorce lawsuit, but God's consistent offer of hope at the end of each section demonstrates the great love that God has for His sinful people.

Adultery in Israel and Hosea's family

In order to teach Hosea and the Israelites the seriousness of the nation's sins and the depth of God's love for His covenant people, God had Hosea marry a prostitute to symbolize God's relationship with the sinful Israelites (1:2). After some time Gomer was unfaithful to Hosea (the third child probably was not Hosea's, contrast 1:3 and 1:6), just like Israel was unfaithful to God. Divorce accusations of adultery were brought against Gomer (2:1,5) and the adultery of worshiping the Canaanite fertility god Baal was charged against Israel (2:8-13). In spite of this terrible sin, Hosea loved Gomer again and God loved Israel again (3:1). On account of God's love, those who were not His people would one day become His people (1:9; 2:23) and His kingdom would be established under a Davidic king (3:5). Through this experience Hosea came to understand the nature of giving undeserved love. He began to see how God felt when the Israelites were unfaithful to their covenant relationship with Him.

Covenant lawsuit against Israel for adultery

God brought three charges against Israel: There is no knowledge of God, no steadfast love, and no truth. The reason the people had no knowledge of God is that the priests in Israel forgot God's word (4:6; 5:4) and ignored His instructions (4:10). Instead they became drunk and had sex with prostitutes at the Baal temples (4:11-14). Because of this God will judge the priests (5:1,2) and bring war on the nation (5:8,14). At the end of this section God makes the surprising offer to heal the people if they will seek Him and desire to know Him (5:15-6:3).

The second accusation is that the people have transgressed God's covenant, murdered (6:7-9), raised up wicked kings (7:5-7; 8:3), made political alliances with other pagan nations (7:8,11; 8:8-10), and worshiped at the golden calves (8:5,6). Each of these accusations shows that Israel has no steadfast love for God. Although God loved them and brought them up from Egypt, they rejected His love (11:1-4). God must discipline them, but because of His deep love He will not give them up. One day they will respond to Him and return to Him (11:8-11).

The third charge is that the nation is full of deception and lies like Jacob their father; there is no truth in them (11:12-12:4). Their worship of Baal was a deception, for there is no other God but the Lord (13:1-4). Although the nation will soon be destroyed, Hosea calls the people to return to God and receive His forgiveness and healing (14:1-4).

Theological significance

1. Sin is not a minor thing to God; it is a betrayal of a love commitment, a prostitution of love to something other than God.
2. In spite of the horribleness of sin, God's love is deeper. He will forgive and heal those who seek and love Him.
3. The difficult circumstances of life can be used by God to strengthen us so that God is glorified through our weakness.
4. A real experiential knowledge of God and His word, a consistent love for God, and truthfulness are central factors of a personal relationship with God.

The New Testament, like Hosea, uses the marriage relationship to describe a person's covenant relationship to God (Eph 5:22-33). Paul and Peter use Hosea 1:10 and 2:23 to demonstrate that God's grace in redeeming the Gentiles was a fulfillment of His plan to make those who were not His people, His people (Rom. 9:25,26; 1 Pet. 2:10). Jesus quoted Hosea 6:6 to explain that God desires steadfast love rather than sacrifices (Matt. 9:13; 12:7).

Notes

1. For information on the history, archeological discoveries and a map of the city of Nineveh, see D. W. Wiseman, "Nineveh," *The Illustrated Bible Dictionary*, Vol. II (Leicester: InterVarsity Press, 1980), p. 1089-92.
2. E. Good, *Irony in the Bible* (Philadelphia: Westminster, 1965), p. 39-55, discusses a number of ironic features in Jonah.
3. P. C. Craigie, "Amos the NOQED in Light of Ugaritic," *Studies in Religion* 11 (1982), p. 29-33, shows that the term "shepherd" in 1:1 refers to a manager of shepherds.
4. G. V. Smith, *Amos: A Commentary* (Grand Rapids: Eerdmans, 1989), p. 188,89, believes Sakkut refers to the Assyrian worship of the god associated with the planet Saturn. This god was considered a king and called Ninurta in some texts.

Discussion questions

1. How do the sovereignty of God and the free will of mankind work together in the story of Jonah?
2. What was wrong with Jonah's understanding of God?
3. What does Amos 1 say about accountability of the heathen?
4. Does God condemn riches in Amos or is it the use of wealth?
5. What did Hosea learn about God through his marriage?

EARLY PROPHETS FROM JUDAH

7

Micah and Isaiah
Time of Ministry: Micah 725-690 B.C.; Isaiah 750-690 B.C.

After the death of Solomon (931 B.C.) and the division of Israel into two nations (see 1 Kings 11-12), the southern nation of Judah suffered under the leadership of a series of kings who did not love God like King David did. Rehoboam built idols and altars to Baal and allowed cultic prostitution to thrive in Judah (1 Kings 14:22-24). Both Kings Asa and Jehoshaphat attempted to eliminate Baalism (1 Kings 15:11-14; 2 Chron. 17:1-6), but this false religion was still flourishing in Judah during the prophetic ministry of Micah and Isaiah because Kings Ahaz and Manasseh encouraged it (2 Kings 16; 21; Isa. 7).

Micah and Isaiah lived through four very different time periods, under four quite different kings of Judah. When Isaiah first began to prophesy, Uzziah (called Azariah in 2 Kings 15:1-7) was the powerful and prosperous king of Judah. God blessed all that he did, but later he became very proud and was struck with leprosy (2 Chron. 26:3-21). Isaiah condemned the proud (Isa. 2:11-19) and Judah's preoccupation with wealth (Isa. 3:16-26).

When the wicked King Ahaz came to power in Judah (2 Kings 16), he worshiped foreign gods and refused to trust God for help; therefore, God allowed the Assyrian King Tiglath-pileser III to make Judah his vassal as Isaiah and Micah prophesied (Mic. 1:12-16; Isa. 7). His son, the godly Judean King Hezekiah, removed the idols from Judah and rebelled against the Assyrians. Being hopelessly outnumbered, Hezekiah put his total trust in God. In response, God sent an angel to destroy the Assyrian army and deliver Judah (Isa. 36,37; 2 Kings 18,19).

In spite of Hezekiah's great love for God, his son Manasseh began to reintroduce Baalism into the nation (2 Kings 21). The righteous were persecuted and social relationships were undermined by distrust among relatives and violence against the weak (Mic. 7:1-6). Micah and Isaiah brought messages of hope to the

48

people of Judah during these dark days. God will not abandon His people, and one day will come and restore His kingdom.

Micah
God is coming for you

Micah was from Moresheth-gath, a Judean city near the old Philistine stronghold of Lachish, but he proclaimed most of his prophetic messages in the capital city of Jerusalem. He began his ministry before the fall of Samaria in 722/21 B.C. and received new messages from God until the early years of Manasseh.

The prophet's messages can be divided into three major sections. Each section begins with warnings of judgment and ends with a message of salvation and hope.

Outline of Micah

God will come with great power	Micah 1:1-2:13
He will judge Israel and Judah	1:1-16
Reasons for God's judgment	2:1-11
God will gather a remnant	2:12-13
New leadership will come to Jerusalem	3:1-5:15
God will remove evil leaders	3:1-12
Zion will have a new leader	4:1-5:15
The people must come to God	6:1-7:20
Coming with proper worship	6:1-16
Coming with hope, not despair	7:1-20

Some of these messages are divine judgment speeches (3:1-4), while others are oracles of salvation about the Messiah and the establishment of God's kingdom (4:1-5:5). There is a lament concerning the terrible conditions in Judah (7:1-7), as well as a covenant lawsuit against Judah (6:1-16).

God will come with great power

Early in Micah's ministry (before 722/21 B.C.) he saw a glorious theophany of God coming forth in power from a temple in heaven (1:2-4). God was coming to destroy the idols, false temples, and the capital city of Samaria in Israel. Micah also saw and lamented the coming destruction of Judah (1:8-16). Using the names of towns to create puns, he warned that the "dust town" Beth-le-aphrah will roll in the dust, the "deceptive" Achzib will be deceived, and calamity from God will fall on Jerusalem. Why will this happen? Because the powerful landlords in Judah covet and steal property from the poor (2:1-4,9), because the people think that God is patient and will never punish them (2:6,7), and because the nation is following drunken false prophets (2:11).

In spite of this sure and severe judgment, God will not reject the righteous remnant of Judah. One day He will gather them together; their king will lead them to freedom (2:12,13).

New leadership will come to Jerusalem

In order to transform Judah, God needed to remove the present evil leadership in Judah (Ahaz and other high officials in government). Those who were ruling unjustly by savagely mistreating others will be treated in a similar manner by their enemies (3:1-4,9,10). Money-hungry prophets and priests were more concerned with their profits than giving spiritual direction from God. They were not filled with God's Spirit like Micah, so they foolishly taught that God would never judge Judah. They refused to boldly condemn the people for their sins (3:5-8,11).

In the last days new leadership will come to Jerusalem and God Himself will reign as king over Zion (4:1,7). At that time the poor and weak, as well as foreigners from all the nations, will come to Jerusalem to be instructed by God (4:2,6,7). All war will end and prosperity will fill the earth (4:3-5). Although the nation will first go through the excruciating pain of exile in Babylon (4:9-11), a new and powerful ruler (the Messiah) will be born in Bethlehem (5:2). He will bring peace to all the world, restore the remnant of Judah, and remove all those earthly things (military might, strong cities, false gods, and false prophets) that people put their trust in (5:4-15).

The people must come to God

During the final years of Hezekiah, Manasseh began to introduce his pagan ways into the nation. Micah declared God's covenant lawsuit¹ against Judah because they forgot that God had delivered them from Egypt and reversed the curse of Balaam (6:1-4). They thought that they could please God by going through the ritual of many sacrifices, but God requires that people act justly, love kindness and walk humbly with God (6:6-8). God will destroy these unjust, violent, and deceptive people (6:9-16).

Living during the early years of Manasseh was depressing even for a prophet of God. Micah lamented because it seemed that the godly people had perished, violence was everywhere, and no one could be trusted (7:1-6). But suddenly he remembered that God is a God of salvation. He hears and answers prayer (7:7,8). Although some mocked Micah (7:10), he remained confident that the people of Judah will one day return and rebuild Jerusalem after their exile (7:11,12). God will shepherd them back to their land just as He did when they came out of Egypt (7:14-17). Remembering this he praised God, for God's unchanging love brings forgiveness of sins and His everlasting compassion knows no end (7:18-20).

Theological significance

1. God will bring judgment on those who do not rule by justice.
2. Teachers who depend on God's patience or think that God will never judge sin are not filled with the Spirit of the Lord.
3. Meaningless ritual is useless. God wants His people to have humble hearts and behavior that is just and kind to others.
4. It is possible to have hope in the midst of oppression and violence if trust is put in God and His promises.
5. The Messiah was born in Bethlehem as Micah said (Matt. 2:3-6) and one day He will reign as king over all the earth. All war will end and people from all nations will worship Him.

Isaiah

The Holy One will bring judgment and redemption

Isaiah's earliest prophecies were given near the end of the reign of Uzziah (ca. 750 B.C.) and continued until the beginning of Manasseh's co-regency with Hezekiah (ca. 690 B.C.), thus paralleling most of Micah's ministry. Isaiah was married and had at least two children (7:3; 8:3). He lived in Jerusalem and from time to time he spoke to the kings of Judah (Isa. 7; 39). He delivered prophecies of judgment and salvation about Judah, as well as many foreign nations (Isa. 13-27). He is best known for his messianic prophecies about both a king and a suffering servant (Isa. 9; 53). His writings are infiltrated with his sense of the holiness of God because his life was forever changed once he saw the glory of God, the almighty king sitting on His throne (Isa. 6). His messages are organized into major blocks.

Outline of Isaiah

The exaltation of God humbles man's pride	Isaiah 1-6
The prince of peace will end Judah's wars	7-12
God's sovereign plan for the nations	13-27
Trusting God or military might	28-39
The incomparable God will bring deliverance	40-48
The suffering servant will bring salvation	49-55
God's final restoration and judgment	56-66

Isaiah was a gifted preacher who used elaborate illustrations (Judah is a vineyard in chap. 5) and interesting figures of speech (Judah's kings are called the rulers of Sodom in 1:10). His messages were bold declarations of the power of God to save people from sin and to deliver kings from stronger political rulers. He called the nation to trust God because there is no other God. God will establish His kingdom forever.

The exaltation of God humbles man's pride

Isaiah called the rebellious people of Judah who had suffered military disaster to repent, act justly, and cease offering meaningless ritual in the temple (1:1-20). God will remove the nation's oppressive leaders and the proud rich women who lived during the prosperous reign of Uzziah (3:1-4:1). He will destroy His precious vineyard which produced no good fruit (5:1-7). Then in the last days God will humble all proud people when His glory is revealed on earth (2:2,3,10-17). Jerusalem will be transformed, the Branch of God (the Messiah) will be there, sins will be removed, and Jerusalem will be holy (4:2-6).

In the year Uzziah died, Isaiah saw a vision of the glory of the holy King of Kings sitting upon His throne in the temple. Isaiah humbled himself, was forgiven, and sent by God to harden the hearts of those who refused to listen to God (6:1-13).[2]

The prince of peace will end Judah's wars

During the reign of the wicked King Ahaz, Judah was attacked by Syria and Israel. Ahaz refused to trust in God for deliverance (7:1-19), but instead sought help from Assyria; even though God foretold the demise of Israel and Syria (8:1-7; 9:8-10:4) as well as the arrogant Assyrians (10:5-19). In this hopeless situation God offered hope and peace through Immanuel,[3] the son born to the virgin (7:14); through the great Light, the Prince of Peace who would rule forever on the throne of David (9:1-7; see Matt. 4:13-16); and through the shoot or branch who was filled with God's Spirit (11:1-9). These promises will cause people to trust in the God of their salvation and thank Him (12:1-6).

God's sovereign plan for the nations

Because the nations became quite proud of their riches and military might (13:11,19; 16:6; 23:9), Isaiah's war oracles against the nations prophesied the fall of Babylon, Assyria, Philistia, Moab, Syria, Egypt, Edom, Arabia, and Tyre (13-23). On the day of the Lord, these nations will be destroyed when the wrath of God burns against them (13:6-13). No one can frustrate this plan, nor God's plan to establish Judah back in its land (14:1-3; 16:5). Surprisingly, we read that many Gentiles from Egypt and Assyria will respond to God and become part of the people of God (19:19-25). Isaiah's words encouraged those Jews who were uncertain about their future. The pagan nations were not to be feared. God's plan for the world will be fulfilled.

These events will foreshadow the final day of judgment when God will destroy everything on the earth with fire. Because of wickedness, God will punish men, kings, and proud cities (24:1-22). At that time He will reign with His people in Zion and be exalted. Death and tears will end and all will sing for joy at the lavish banquet of God. The dead will be brought to life; joy and salvation will cover the earth (25:1-26:19).

Trusting God or military might

Isaiah moves from God's final plans for the earth to the situation in Israel just before it fell in 722/21 B.C. He contrasted the proud drunken leaders of Israel (kings, priests, and prophets), who refused to be taught, with God who rules with perfect justice and gives true instruction to the remnant of the nation (28:1-29). They will be destroyed, and Judah too, for Judah did not learn from Israel's mistakes. Their prophets also will deceive them. The people will give lip service to God but their hearts will be far from Him (29:9-14). One of the chief evidences of this was the leaders' tendency to depend on Egypt for security from the Assyrians (30:1-4; 31:1-3). They did not want to trust in God or the prophet's words (30:9-12). Isaiah condemned this worthless trust in the flesh. In compassion God desired to teach Judah, bless them with prosperity, and deliver them from the Assyrians, but they must first return to Him and trust Him (30:18-31:9). To encourage this faith, Isaiah reminded the people that one day their righteous messianic king would come and remove their blindness (32:1-8). He called the complacent women to mourn the coming danger (32:9-14) and he prophesied the exaltation of God when the fierce Assyrians will be destroyed by Judah's majestic King (33:1-24). Edom and all God's enemies will face the wrath of God (34:1-15) but there will be joy in Jerusalem when the ransomed return to dwell in Zion (35:1-10).

Hezekiah accepted this message and placed his total trust in God when the Assyrian army surrounded the city of Jerusalem (36:1-22). Although human reason would suggest that Hezekiah should surrender, Hezekiah and Isaiah went to the temple and prayed that God would defeat the Assyrians and thus declare His glory to all the nations of the earth (37:14-20). God answered this prayer and an angel killed 185,000 Assyrian troups that night (37:36). Because of Hezekiah's righteous life and his prayer to God, his life was lengthened by 15 years (38:1-22). In spite of his earlier faith, later Hezekiah made an alliance with the Babylonians rather than trusting God totally (39:1-8).

The incomparable God will bring deliverance

Although these chapters are not dated, they were probably given in the last days of Hezekiah when his wicked son Manasseh began to rule. Through these prophecies God encouraged the faithful remnant to maintain their trust in God, for He would deliver them from future exile in Babylon. Comfort is given because God is coming with power to rule His people (40:1-11). Since no nation or foreign god has even a fraction of the power of God, they need not be feared (40:12-26). Though the people were confused and blind to the power of God, there was hope in the Lord (40:27; 41:10; 42:18-20). If God's people will wait and trust in Him, they will never lack strength (40:27-31).

God disputed the claims of other pagan nations and their gods. Their gods can do nothing; they are just nicely carved pieces of wood that some man made (41:5-7,21-24; 44:9-20). The Babylonian gods Bel (called Marduk by the Babylonians) and Nebo will fall and Babylon will also (46:1-47:15). There is no other God beside the God of Judah. He is the first and the last, the Holy one, the Creator, the Savior and King (41;4; 43:10-15; 44:6-8; 48:12). He knows all about the former things that happened in ancient history and has planned out the future for His people (43:18-21).

After Judah goes into exile God will raise up a powerful king who will defeat many nations. That king, Cyrus, will allow the Jews to return home from Babylon and enable Jerusalem and God's temple to be rebuilt (41:1-4; 44:24-45:7; 48:20; see the fulfillment in Ezra 1:1-6). This shows that God still loves them, for He chose them to be His servants. They will be God's witnesses to declare His glory among the nations.

The suffering servant will bring salvation

Isaiah drew a contrast between the Jews who were God's disobedient servants (42:19) and another servant that was chosen by God to establish justice and righteousness on the earth (42:1-4). Although He will toil in vain among His own people, in the end He will be a light to the nations so that God's salvation may reach to the ends of the earth (42:6; 49:4,6). At first He will be despised and humiliated (46:7; 50:6), His face will be disfigured, He will willingly die for the sins of others (52:14; 53:3-8). In the midst of this He will look to God for help and God will raise Him from the dead and greatly exalt Him (50:7-10; 52:13; 53:12). He will be a guilt offering to God to bear the sins of the world even though He was sinless (53:9-11). This exalted suffering servant is the messianic king, the Jesus of the New Testament (Mark 10:33,34; John 10:17,18; Acts 8:32-35).[4]

God not only promised to save His people from their sins but He encouraged them to seek the Lord, pay attention to the law, and enjoy His deliverance (51:1-3). Their exile will soon be over, He will restore His faithful remnant to Zion and it will be like a beautiful garden. Then the people will break forth into singing, proclaiming, "Thy God reigneth," when God delivers Jerusalem (52:1-10). The barren and rejected city of Jerusalem will overflow with people and joy because of God's everlasting love for His people (54:1-8). If they will only seek the Lord and forsake their wicked ways, God will pardon their sins (55:6-8). Although His marvelous ways are far beyond human understanding, His word will be accomplished according to the everlasting covenant with David (55:1-13).

God's final restoration and judgment

The ethics of God's new restored kingdom will be characterized by justice, the proper observance of the Sabbath (56:1-8), humble fasting which delights in God and reaches out to the needs of the oppressed (58:1-12), and a turning from the iniquities that separated people from God (59:1-3). When the glory of the Lord will rise as a light of salvation for His people, the nations will come to Jerusalem to worship and give gifts to Him (60:1-9). God will change their sorrows into joy, their deserts into gardens, their ruins into rebuilt cities. The nation will be called Zion of the Holy One of Israel, my delight is in her, the holy people (62:1-12). The servant will proclaim the acceptable day of the Lord, freedom from prison, a day of joy and praise for all who mourn (61:1-3). These events will also include a final day of judgment on Edom and all the nations, for God's fierce wrath will trample down all who reject Him (63:1-7).

The prophecies of Isaiah end with a prayer of praise to God for His lovingkindness in saving them from past affliction, a confession of sin and rebellion against the Holy Spirit, and a petition that God would again reveal His power and glory to His people and not be angry with them anymore (63:7-64:12). God answered this prayer with a promise to reveal Himself to all those who seek Him and turn from sinfulness and to act on behalf of His faithful servants by pouring out His blessings on this new heaven and earth that He will create (65:1-25). In the end, all the wicked will dwell in a place of eternal fire where the worms do not die, but all the rest of the nations will see the glory of God and all will bow down before Him (66:18-24).

Theological significance

1. God hates pride and loves the humble. Pride will be destroyed and God alone will be exalted.

2. God is sovereignly in control of all the nations of the earth. He uses some nations as instruments in His hand to punish other nations. God delivers nations that put their total trust in Him rather than alliances or military power.

3. God will send His Immanuel, the prince of peace, the messianic king on David's throne, to deliver God's people and establish His kingdom of prosperity, peace, and joy.

4. God is the first and the last, the Creator, Savior and Holy One of Israel, yet He cares for His own. All the power of the nations is like nothing before Him.

5. The suffering servant paid the penalty for the sins of the world through His death and exaltation. He is a light to all nations and through Him many Jews and Gentiles will be holy and enjoy the glorious kingdom of God.

Notes

1. H. B. Huffmon, "The Covenant Lawsuit in the Prophets," *Journal of Biblical Literature* 78 (1959), p. 285-95.
2. Jesus quoted these verses (Matt. 13:14-17), realizing that one of the purposes of His ministry was to harden the hearts of unbelievers. This does not deny people's free choice to repent, but if repentance is repeatedly rejected, God may give them over to their depraved minds and harden their hearts (Rom. 1:18-32).
3. Because of the context (7:15-17) some believe that this prophecy was fulfilled when a virgin of Ahaz' day gave birth to a child by natural means. Others believe there was a double fulfillment, one in Ahaz' day and one when Christ was born. Some think that 7:14 refers only to Jesus' birth. Isaiah 7:15-17 refers to the time it takes a child to know what is right and wrong (possibly 3 years) as a measure for when the Assyrians will control Ahaz and Judah.
4. The first two chapters in H. H. Rowley, *The Servant of the Lord and Other Essays in the Old Testament* (London: Nelson, 1952), survey various ways people have interpreted this passage.

Discussion questions

1. What are some of the characteristics of a true prophet (Mic. 3:8) and the false prophets in Micah's day?
2. Why was Micah so discouraged (Mic. 7:1-6)? How did focusing on God's power help him overcome his depression?
3. What factors caused Isaiah (Isa. 6) to be willing to go wherever God sent him? Did Isaiah expect to win many converts?
4. What evidence in Isaiah 19, 45, 49, 60, and 66 suggests that God's missionary purpose was to win people of all nations?
5. How does the New Testament relate the prophecies of Isaiah 7:14; 9:1-7; 49:6; 52:13-53:12; 61:1-3 to the life of Jesus?

LATE PRE-EXILIC PROPHETS

8

Nahum, Zephaniah, Habakkuk, Joel
Time of Ministry: Nahum 630 B.C.; Zephaniah 625 B.C.; Habakkuk 607 B.C.; Joel 590 B.C.

The events that led to the destruction of Judah in 587/86 B.C. and its exile in Babylon were directly related to the nation's inept political leadership and its religious apostasy. Manasseh did not trust God but submitted to the powerful Assyrians and rebuilt the idols and pagan places of worship which Hezekiah destroyed (2 Kings 21). Later Josiah (640-609 B.C.) began to seek the Lord in his eighth year (632 B.C.), tore down some pagan altars in his 12th year, and carried out a great revival in his 18th year when the Law of Moses was discovered in the temple (2 Chron. 34,35). When the Assyrians were defeated at Nineveh (612 B.C.), Egypt took control of Judah. A few years later (605 B.C.) Babylon defeated Egypt and took Jewish captives to Babylon. More captives went to Babylon when the evil kings Jehoiakim and his son Jehoiachin returned to the pagan ways of Manasseh and were defeated at Jerusalem in 597 B.C. (2 Kings 23:36-24:17). The last king of Judah, Zedekiah, followed this same pattern and eventually the Babylonians returned to destroy the temple and all of Jerusalem. Nebuchadnezzar took all but the very old and injured away into Babylonian captivity (2 Kings 24:18-25:12).

Nahum
God's wrath on Nineveh

Nahum came from the Judean village of Elkosh to preach a message of encouragement to Josiah and the people of Judah. Although God was gracious to the Assyrians after they responded positively to the preaching of Jonah over 150 years earlier, before long they went back to their old ways. The Assyrians, whose capital was Nineveh, oppressed Judah and many other countries. Many righteous people began to wonder if God would ever destroy the Assyrians as Isaiah prophesied (Isa. 10:5-34). God revealed to Nahum that He still was an all powerful God who executes judgment against evil and is good to those who trust Him. These prophecies encouraged Josiah not to submit to the Assyrians but to move forward with his political and religious reforms.

Outline of Nahum

God's judgment of Nineveh	Nahum 1:1-2:2
God's wrath and goodness	1:1-8
Wrath on Nineveh, peace to Judah	1:9-2:2
The destruction of Nineveh	2:3-13
Reasons for Nineveh's inevitable doom	3:1-19

The vividness of Nahum's description of the battle for Nineveh and his knowledge of the geography of the rivers flowing beside and through the city of Nineveh suggest that the prophet was very aware of military tactics of his time. But the essence of his message was not based as much on his knowledge of Assyria as on his knowledge of the character of God.

God's judgment of Nineveh

Nahum began his prophecy with a poem that reminded his listeners of God's wrath, His power, and His goodness (1:1-8) because it is impossible to understand God's ways apart from His character. He is a holy God who requires holy living. Although He is slow to anger, He will not leave His enemies unpunished. He is also a God of great power. Not even the mountains can stand when His wrath is poured out like fire. This power will also protect those who trust in God in times of trouble (1:7,8).

These theological truths apply directly to Judah's situation. God's power will bring a complete end to the Assyrian enemies of God (1:9-11). Though they are very strong, God is stronger and will bring an army to destroy their reputations and their idols (1:14; 2:1). Judah will then be free, peace will come, and Judah will again celebrate and worship God (1:13,15).

The destruction of Nineveh

The siege and capture of the Assyrian capital of Nineveh is described in brilliant pictures. Speeding chariots, clashing swords, terrified red-dressed soldiers, tumbling walls near the river, looting of the palace riches, fleeting troops, and weeping women are part of the battle scene. Although the Assyrians roared around the ancient Near East like a vicious lion, God will cut off their strength and military might (2:11-13).

This prophecy would have seemed very unlikely in Nahum's day because the Assyrian king Ashurbanipal was the most powerful of all the Assyrians kings. History and archeological excavations suggest that the city did fall in 612 B.C. and that it was partially due to a flood just like Nahum predicted (2:6,8).[1]

Reasons for Nineveh's inevitable doom

To encourage faith in those who heard this prophecy, God explained why He was erasing Nineveh from the map. It was a violent and bloody city; they killed innocent people by the thousands in their military conquests (3:1-4). Because of this God will disgrace them, throw filth in their faces, and totally devastate the city. Though many thought Nineveh was impregnable, it will be defeated just like the impregnable Egyptian city of Thebes which the Assyrians defeated in 663 B.C. (3:8-12).

Nahum ends his prophecy with a taunt against the Assyrians (3:14-19). He mockingly encourages them to draw some water (with the flood, that was the last thing they needed), to fortify the wall with some new bricks (it was too late to do this after the wall had fallen), and to multiply themselves like grasshoppers (but grasshoppers just hide or fly away). When people hear about the fall of Nineveh, they will rejoice and clap their hands.

Theological significance

1. God sovereignly rules the nations of this world. Some will receive His wrath, but He will be good to those who trust Him.
2. Military power and riches will not deliver a sinful nation from the power of God's destruction. No nation is indestructible.
3. God was gracious to the Assyrians when Jonah preached to them, but Nahum indicates that God's patience lasts only so long.

Paul saw that the joy at the announcement of the good news of peace in Nahum's day (1:15) was similar to the joy when the good news of Christ was proclaimed in his day (Rom. 10:15).

Zephaniah
The day of the Lord

The prophet Zephaniah lived before the major reform of King Josiah (621 B.C.) for idolatry, violence, and false prophets still existed (1:1-6; 3:1-4). The reference to a "remnant of Baal" in 1:4 may suggest that Josiah had made some initial attempts to remove Baalism from Jerusalem (628 B.C.) but that the task was not complete. If this prophecy is dated about 625 B.C., Josiah would have just declared independence from Assyria (627 B.C.) and was in need of encouragement in his religious reforms. The prophet warns about the coming day of the Lord.

The idea of the day of the Lord comes from the belief that God is a divine warrior who fights holy wars against His enemies. When He comes in power to defeat the wicked, He also delivers His own people. The day of the Lord is a day of victory and joy for those who love God, but a day of destruction for unbelievers.[2]

God's judgment on the day of the Lord

Zephaniah warned that God would come and devastate the earth, removing man, beasts, birds, and fish. This judgment was particularly aimed at Judah because some people were still worshiping the Canaanite god Baal, bowing down to the Ammonite god Milcom (or Molech), and praying to Assyrian astral deities (1:4,5; cf. Jer. 8:2; 19:13). People were rejecting the reform movement of Josiah, refusing to turn to God, and continuing in the pagan worship introduced earlier by Manasseh.

Zephaniah claimed that the day of the Lord was not just a divine punishment which applied to the pagans who worshiped idols. God's wrath would soon fall on all who refused to follow Him, even the Jews. God will slaughter them like a sacrifice, both the royal princes who have accepted foreign customs and the violent criminals who deceive and steal (1:7-9). Every part of Jerusalem will be affected, even the rich part of town (1:10-13).

To show how serious the danger was, Zephaniah reminded his listeners of the horribleness of the day of the Lord (1:14-18). It will be a day when tough soldiers will cry, when people will walk around aimlessly like blind people, when rich people will not be able to buy security. Wrath, distress, destruction, and blood will be everywhere. It will be like hell on earth.

Repent before the day of the Lord

The good news is that it is possible for Judah to avoid the judgment side of the day of the Lord. Zephaniah exhorted the people to gather at the temple and repent before the anger of the Lord falls on them (2:1-3). If they humble themselves, seek God's face, and follow His ways, God may be gracious to them.

God revealed a second reason why they should repent. The Philistines, Moabites, Ammonites, and arrogant Assyrians will be defeated and the faithful remnant of the Jews will receive their land (2:4-15). Eventually all people will bow before Judah's God (2:11), so why would anyone from Judah want to worship worthless pagan gods and be destroyed like the heathen? Although God hoped that Judah would fear Him and follow His ways

(3:7), they did not trust God because their political and religious leaders profaned the temple and preached that God would never judge them (3:1-5).

Restoration and joy on the day of the Lord
If the people will repent then they will be a part of the righteous remnant from all over the world that has purified lips, forgiven sins, humble attitudes, and holy lives (3:9-13). These people will rejoice because God their king will dwell in their midst (3:14,15). God will also rejoice over His people who were weak and oppressed, but now are gathered together and blessed.

Theological significance
1. No sinner, no matter what nationality or religion, can avoid the wrath of God's judgment on the day of the Lord.
2. Those who repent and humble themselves will be purified and have the blessing of enjoying God's presence forever.

Habakkuk
Resolving questions about God's justice

The prophet Habakkuk prophesied after the fall of Nineveh in 612 B.C. but before the surprising rise of the Babylonian kingdom under Nebuchadnezzar in 605 B.C. This places Habakkuk in Judah around 607 B.C. during the reign of the wicked king Jehoiakim (2 Kings 23:34-24:17). Because Habakkuk's final prayer was set to music for singing in the temple (3:1,19), some believe the prophet may have also served as a levitical singer in the temple (1 Chron. 25:1-8).[3] His book is organized by his three prayers.

Outline of Habakkuk

A prayer for God's justice in Judah	Hab. 1:1-11
A prayer questioning God's justice	1:12-2:20
A prayer for mercy in a time of difficulty	3:1-19

Habakkuk struggled with some of the same problems that Job did. Neither man doubted the power or holiness of God but neither understood how a God of justice could allow certain things to happen. Both received a new vision of God and both trusted God's wisdom in spite of very difficult situations.

A prayer for God's justice in Judah
The early years of Jehoiakim's reign were full of violence, strife, wickedness, injustice, and the oppression of the righteous (1:1-4). In his prayer Habakkuk questions why God allowed this evil to go unpunished and why He did not save the righteous who served God so faithfully during the reign of Josiah.

God's answer revealed that He would demonstrate His justice in a surprising way (1:5-11). The state of Babylon would amazingly rise to power and invade Judah, violently bringing about the justice Habakkuk desired by killing the violent people in Judah. No one will be able to stop this fierce military machine; it will be as fast as a leopard. They will mock the power of Judah's puny king and crush him.

A prayer questioning God's justice

Though God's reply answered Habakkuk's original question, this divine plan raised even greater questions. How could the holy everlasting divine Rock who promised to protect His people (1:12) give His approval to the wicked Babylonians by allowing them to destroy the more righteous nation of Judah (1:13).

Habakkuk waited and God gave a twofold answer that the prophet was to record on a tablet so that all could see it (2:1-3). First, the righteous person must live by faith in God in times of difficulty (2:4). Since God's mysterious ways are often beyond human understanding, Habakkuk must trust God. Secondly, God indicates that the proud Babylonians who looted nations with violence, who thrived on drunkenness, and worshiped idols of stone were not receiving God's approval (2:4-19). They will be cut off and violence will overtake them, for one day the glory of the Lord will fill the earth (2:14).

A prayer for mercy in a time of difficulty

Habakkuk was assured by God's answer, but that did not remove the difficulty of going through the terrible wars with Babylon. He pleaded that God would be merciful while pouring out His wrath (3:2). The prophet's faith was strengthened as he remembered the glorious power of God in the past. Nothing could stand before His anger when He marched through the earth to save His people (3:12,13). Realizing the power of God, Habakkuk trembled at the thought of the upcoming destruction. Yet his heart rejoiced and the load on his feet was removed as he placed his life in the strong hands of God (3:17-19).

Theological significance

1. God's ways are sometimes mysterious but they are guided by His character. Justice on earth does not mean that the innocent will never suffer, but God will be with those who suffer.
2. The just shall live by faith. God's power and past mercy give strength to face present difficulties with joy.

The New Testament writers used Habakkuk's statement that the just shall live by faith (Rom. 1:17; Gal. 3:11; Heb. 10:37) not through works. Abraham (Gen. 15:6) and Habakkuk (2:4) make it very clear that no one can work their way into heaven. Salvation is solely by grace through faith (Eph. 2:8-10).

Joel
The day of the Lord is near and in the future

Joel prophesied shortly before the fall of Jerusalem in 587/86 B.C. People from Judah had been taken into captivity in Babylon in 605 and 597 B.C. (3:1-3) but the temple in Jerusalem had not yet been destroyed (2:16,17). Around 590 B.C., Joel taught that the severe grasshopper plague was a warning from God that the day of the Lord, the final day of Judah, was very near.

Outline of Joel

Repent because of the present day of the Lord	Joel 1:1-2:17
Lament because of the locust	1:1-20
Repent because military destruction is near	2:1-17
Grace and wrath on the future day of the Lord	2:18-3:21
Restoration and the Spirit	2:18-32
Judgment of the nations	3:1-17
Blessings on Judah	3:18-21

It is difficult to determine whether the description of the army of locusts in 2:1-17 is to be understood literally, a position that seems to make chapter 2 a repetition of chapter 1, or if this is a description of the coming Babylonian army, using the imagery of grasshoppers. Since the locusts in chapter 1 have already come and those in 2 will come in the near future, chapter 2 probably refers to the Babylonian army.[4]

Repent because of the present day of the Lord

A very unusual event happened, something that fathers would tell their sons about for years. Judah had an unbelievable infestation of grasshoppers. They were everywhere and eating everything in sight. Everyone was weeping because there would be no wine, no figs, no grain for offerings at the temple, no harvest for the farmers, and no fruit on the trees (1:4-12).

Joel did not interpret this plague as a freak of nature but as a warning from God. He encouraged the priests to call the people together at the temple, start a fast in sackcloth, and cry out to God for help (1:13,14). They should lament because when there is no grain in the barns and no water in the rivers, it is a sure sign that the day of the Lord is very near (1:17-20).

Joel pictured this day of the Lord as a great military invasion, similar to an invasion of grasshoppers (2:1-17). These creatures will invade the land by the thousands and nothing will be able to stop them. It will be the great and awesome day of the Lord when Judah will be destroyed (fulfilled in 587/86 B.C.). The only hope is for the people to gather at the temple (2:14-17), return to God, weep, and fast. It is possible that God might be patient a little longer and gracious even though the people do not deserve it (2:12-13).

Grace & wrath on the future day of the Lord

Joel balances his words of judgment in the near future with words of hope on the final day of the Lord. The locust plague will be reversed on that day because the locusts and northern army of Babylonians will be gone (2:20,25), abundant grain will be in the fields, there will be joy and no more shame. God will pour out His Spirit on all flesh in a new way and whoever calls on the name of the Lord will be saved (2:28-32). Judah will be restored from captivity and the nations will be judged (3:1-8).

God will sit as judge over all the nations on that final day of the Lord (3:9-14). Then all will know that He alone is God, for He will dwell in Zion and it will be a holy place (3:17,21).

Theological significance

1. The only way to avoid the judgment of God is to repent with all your heart and trust in God's mercy.
2. On the final day of the Lord, God will judge the wicked and bless the righteous with his presence.

Peter taught that Joel's prophecy of the outpouring of the Spirit on all flesh (Acts 2:17-21; Joel 2:28-32) began to be fulfilled at Pentecost. Paul taught that it was necessary to call on the name of the Lord to be saved (Rom. 10:13; Joel 2:32).

Notes

1. C. J. Gadd, *The Fall of Nineveh* (London: British Museum, 1923), p. 25-30, and H. W. F. Saggs, "Nahum and the Fall of Nineveh," *Journal of Theological Studies* 20 (1969), p. 220-225, discuss these issues.
2. M. Weiss, "The Origin of the Day of the Yahweh Reconsidered," *Hebrew Union College Annual* 37 (1966), p. 29-72, discusses various possible ways of interpreting the day of the Lord.
3. R. L. Smith, *Micah-Malachi* (Waco: Word, 1984), p. 93, but this is only an educated guess.
4. D. Stuart, *Hosea-Jonah* (Waco: Word, 1987), p. 232-34.

Discussion questions

1. How can God be a God of both wrath and goodness?
2. Is it appropriate for believers to question the justice of God? How can one overcome doubt in difficult times?
3. Describe the day of the Lord for the righteous in Zephaniah 3:9-20?
4. How does Joel help to reveal the nature of true repentance?

LATE PRE-EXILIC PROPHETS

9

Jeremiah, Lamentations, Obadiah
Time of Ministry: Jeremiah 627-580 B.C.; Obadiah 585 B.C.

Jeremiah served as God's prophet to Judah with Zephaniah during the reign of the righteous King Josiah, with Habakkuk during the reign of the wicked King Jehoiakim, and with Joel during the reign of Zedekiah, the last king of Judah (see chapter 8). A few years after Zedekiah came to the throne (597 B.C.) he rebelled against Nebuchadnezzar.

Soon the Babylonians laid siege to Jerusalem and in 587/86 B.C. the city and temple were burnt (2 Kings 24:18-25:21). Some Jews fled to the nearby country of Edom to escape from the war, others died in the fighting, and most of those left were taken into captivity in Babylon. Nebuchadnezzar made Gedaliah the new governor of the people left in Judah, but soon he was killed and the remaining Jews fled to Egypt (Jer. 40-44).

Jeremiah
Overcoming deception and persecution

Jeremiah was from a priestly family that lived in Anathoth, a city of Benjamin just four miles northeast of Jerusalem (1:1). Jeremiah suffered great persecution at the hand of Judah's last two kings and his own extended family tried to kill him (11:18-23). He struggled with why God was making him go through such bitter experiences. He cried out in frustration with several laments (12:1-6; 15:10-21; 18:19-23; 20:1-13). Through all these hardships Jeremiah came to realize that nothing was too difficult for God to accomplish (32:17,18).

Outline of Jeremiah

Prophecies and prayers of Jeremiah	Jer. 1-20
Early calls for repentance	1-9
Exhortations and laments	10-20
Warnings concerning the fall of Jerusalem	21-29
Promises of hope and restoration	30-33
The final days of Jerusalem	34-45
Exile in Egypt	40-45
God's judgment on the foreign nations	46-51
Historical account of the fall of Jerusalem	52

Of all the prophets, Jeremiah was the most open about his own personal struggles with his calling to preach, his difficulty with false prophets who deceived the people with words of peace (28,29), and his frustration over the beatings and imprisonment that he endured (20:1-6; 37:1-38:28). His prayers reveal his disappointment with the nation's unwillingness to repent and his agony over the deceptive ways of the nation (7:1-15; 8:18-9:1). In spite of this, Jeremiah had a deep love for his people, even though they were full of idolatry and about to be destroyed.

Prophecies and prayers of Jeremiah

Jeremiah was chosen to be God's prophet before his birth. Although he did not feel adequate for the responsibility of speaking God's positive and negative words (1:6-10), God strengthened him and promised to make him as secure as a fortified city against those who would oppose him (1:17-19).

In his early preaching during the reign of Josiah, Jeremiah contrasted the nation's original love for God and special holy relationship to God (2:2,3) with their present ignorance of God's law, their rampant Baalism, and their deceptive belief that they had done nothing wrong (2:4-37). He challenged them to admit their sins and return to God so that he could establish the messianic kingdom in Jerusalem (3:11-18; 4:1-4). The people claimed to know the way of the Lord and they thought that they were wise. But, they did not act justly or speak truthfully, so God could not pardon their sins (5:1-9; 8:4-9). They did not fear the Lord because the false prophets deceived the people with promises of peace (5:11-13,20-24,30-31; 6:13-15; 8:10-12).

The people were also deceived by their temple worship. They thought that if they came to the temple, everything would be all right.[1] But God required that they amend their ways and stop oppressing the poor, stealing, swearing falsely, and offering sacrifices to Baal (7:1-10). They need to boast in the Lord rather than their riches or might (9:23,24). If they do not change, God will destroy them and the temple (7:14,15). This brought great sorrow to Jeremiah. He mourned because there seemed to be no healing available for Jerusalem (8:18-9:1; 10:19-25).

Later in the reign of King Jehoiakim (609-597 B.C.) Jeremiah castigated the people for their worship of pieces of wood with golden chains (10:1-5). These idols were a deception and could not even walk or talk. God is the King of all nations, a living God, the creator and the inheritance of the Jews. These idols are stupid, a delusion, a mockery of the truth (10:6-16). By worshiping them, the people had broken their covenant relationship with God (11:1-13). Therefore, God forsook them and hated His beloved people and was forced to destroy their land (12:6-13). In tears Jeremiah confessed the nation's sins and pleaded for God's mercy (14:7-22), but the time of judgment was here and God refused to listen to Jeremiah's prayers (14:11; 15:1).

When Jeremiah prophesied the fall of Jerusalem, persecution came his way. After some men from Anathoth tried to kill him, he lamented his vulnerable position (11:18-23), complained about the prosperity of the wicked (12:1-6), and rejected his miserable prophetic calling (15:10-18). God corrected Jeremiah and challenged him to be strong (12:5) and repent of his complaining so that God could again use him as His prophet (15:19-21). Later when Jeremiah was beaten and put in stocks he cried out to the Lord in agony because he could no longer endure all the mockery and violence against him (20:7-11). It almost seemed that God had deceived him when He called him; maybe it would have been better if he had never been born (20:7,14-18).

During this time Jeremiah acted out several symbolic lessons. The worthless loincloth represented the worthless state of Judah (13:1-11), no weeping at the death of Jeremiah's wife pictured what would happen when Judah fell (16:1-9), the potter's forming of a vessel was similar to God's sovereign control over the nation (18:1-12), and the breaking of the pottery symbolized God's breaking of His people (19:1-13).

Warnings concerning the fall of Jerusalem

Most of the narrative describes Jeremiah's dealings with King Jehoiakim or Zedekiah rather than a series of sermons preached by Jeremiah. Jeremiah told Zedekiah that God would destroy Jerusalem and that the only way to survive was to surrender to the Babylonians (21:1-10). The kings of Judah did not rule by justice, instead they shed innocent blood and refused to follow God; therefore, He was determined to destroy them if there was no repentance (22:1-23:2). The righteous remnant (the good figs) would come from those who went into exile (24:1-10). After seventy years some would return to the land (25:12; 29:10). Then God will shepherd His people and send the Messianic king from the line of David to rule them with justice (23:3-8).

God will also remove the deceptive prophets who claimed that the Lord had spoken to them (23:9-40). Some of them tried to kill Jeremiah when he predicted the destruction of the temple (26:1-

19) and later Hananiah and other exilic prophets contradicted Jeremiah's prophecy that the exile would last 70 years (28-29).

Promises of hope and restoration

Jeremiah's words of hope were given near the end of Zedekiah's reign while the city of Jerusalem was under siege by the Babylonians and the people had given up all hope of survival (32:1). When all human strength was gone (30:5-7), God wanted to assure the nation that through His power He would destroy Babylon and restore them after their exile (30:8-11). For now there would be no healing for the incurable wound that God was inflicting on them (30:12-15). In the future God will restore Judah to health, rebuild her cities, and fill the nation with joy (30:17-22). In His lovingkindness God will restore His covenant with them; it will be an everlasting new covenant that will be written on their hearts (31:1-3,31-37). Jeremiah believed God's promises that the nation would return. He knew that nothing was too difficult for God; therefore, in faith he purchased some property in Anathoth from his uncle (32:6-17). Since God created the earth and controls everyone on it, it is possible to believe that God could cleanse the sins of Judah, restore people and joy to the land, set the messianic Branch from the line of David on the throne and reestablish worship in the temple (33:1-22).

The final days of Jerusalem

The armies of Nebuchadnezzar have now surrounded the city of Jerusalem (34:1) and there seems to be little hope. At this time the people made a covenant with God in the temple to release their Jewish slaves, possibly hoping that God might have mercy on them (34:8-16). A short time later when an Egyptian army came up to Palestine, the Babylonian army left Jerusalem to fight them (37:5-11). When the wealthy Jews saw this, they immediately forced the slaves they had freed back into slavery, in spite of the oath they swore to God (34:11). God was very angry with the people because they did not honor or obey God like the Rechabites (35). This was the pattern of the people and kings ever since Jehioakim burnt the scroll which contained the word of the Lord (36).

Since Jeremiah consistently was faithful in announcing God's judgment on Judah, he was falsely accused of treason, beaten, put in prison (37), and later thrown into a well to die. Jeremiah soon sank into the mud up to his armpits, but a godly Ethiopian servant of the king and 30 men pulled Jeremiah out with ropes (38:1-13). Finally enemy troops entered the city and killed many government officials, blinded Zedekiah and destroyed the walls and the houses in the city (39:1-10). In God's grace Jeremiah and the Ethiopian servant of the king were treated kindly because they trusted God (39:11-18).

Exile in Egypt

Gedaliah was the new governor that Nebuchadnezzar set over the Jews who were left in Judah and the people who fled into Edom and Moab before the Babylonians attacked Jerusalem. Before long, Ishmael killed Gedaliah and slaughtered 80 innocent men (40:13-41:3). Fearing the reprisal of the Babylonians, the remainder of the people went to Bethlehem in order to flee to Egypt (41:16-18). Before they left for Egypt, they decided to have Jeremiah pray to see if this was God's will. They swore to do whatever the Lord said, but when Jeremiah told them that God would curse them if they went to Egypt or richly bless them if they trusted God and stayed in Judah, they thought he was lying (40:1-41:3). Consequently God sent a curse on all of them except Baruch (45:1-5) because they disobeyed God's word, went to Egypt, and offered sacrifices to Egyptian gods (43:8-44:30).

God's judgments on the foreign nations

Although Judah was destroyed, God was not trying to teach the people that the foreign nations around them were free of judgment. Judah had a special relationship with God and was held more accountable, but every person in every nation is responsible for their own actions. Judah should put her trust in God, not in any of these nations. God will defeat the powerful armies of the Egyptians with the army of Babylon (46), an overflowing flood of troops will devastate Philistia (47), and catastrophic destruction will bring the proud land of Moab to weeping (48). Ammon, Edom, Syria, Kedar, and Elam will suffer similar destinies when God's sovereign rule takes control of their lands (49). Jeremiah also sent a message with Seriah to the people in Babylon. Even the great nation Babylon will fall (50-51). Then God will return a remnant to Judah (50:28-34).

Historical account of the fall of Jerusalem

The book of Jeremiah ends with a description of the final battle for Jerusalem, a record of the vessels the Babylonians took from the temple, and a note about a Babylonian act of mercy to the Judean King Jehoiachin after 37 years of exile.

Theological significance

1. God strengthens those He calls and gives them His words.
2. When people are deceived by false preaching, false trust in religious places or observances, or the deception that they know what God can or cannot say, then judgment is near.
3. Those who are godly may suffer great persecution, but they must not bow to public, religious, or official pressure. The pressures of ministry may sometimes make one want to quit, but an honest taking of these issues to God in prayer will bring peace.

4. Believers should weep, not rejoice, over God's judgment of the wicked, and intercede for God's mercy.
5. God is sovereignly in control of all things. He can destroy strong nations as well as forgive and restore His people from captivity and weakness. Truly, nothing is too difficult for God.

The description of the new covenant in 31:31-34 is identified with Jesus' death (Heb. 8:7-13; 9:15) since He was the mediator of the new covenant. At the last supper Jesus instituted the communion service and referred to this as a symbol of the new covenant (Luke 22:20; 1 Cor. 11:25).

Lamentations
Both the good and the bad come from God

This book contains five funeral songs which express the people's grief over the fall of Judah and the destruction of the dearly loved city of Jerusalem. Most believe that Jeremiah wrote these songs in 586 B.C, shortly after the Babylonian army desolated and burned the city of Jerusalem.[2] The songs describe the horrible devastation and cruelty that the author saw. They acknowledge that sin caused this action by God and look beyond the present agony to see a God of faithfulness and mercy who is able to restore the nation.

Outline of Lamentations

Grief over the destruction of Jerusalem	Lam. 1
The day of God's anger for sin	2
A prayer for God's compassion	3
The siege of Jerusalem	4
A plea for God's restoration	5

These poems (except chapter 5) are skillfully written in acrostic form with each verse beginning with the next letter of the Hebrew alphabet.[3] The poems are somewhat repetitive, but each has a unique way of mourning the enormous loss and shame that the people felt. Interestingly, the songs do not blame God for this calamity but see him as the just punisher of their sins.

Grief over the destruction of Jerusalem
Judah weeps bitterly because she has become a slave to a foreign nation. Sorrow is everywhere because there will be no worship in Zion, no rulers, priests, or people. They have sinned against God and He abandoned them to their enemies. They plead with God to see the defilement of the temple, to reach out His hand and comfort them in their time of distress, and to punish their enemies.

The day of God's anger for sin

God's fierce anger did not spare Judah. The divine warrior threw down its defenses, shot His arrows, and sent forth His fire against the temple. He destroyed walls, gates, and palaces. Prophets, elders, virgins, and mothers sat in sackcloth and ashes. Her false prophets gave empty visions and her enemies sneered and laughed. Oh, that God would look and see the weeping, the death, the barbarity, the pain of enduring the anger of God.

A prayer for God's compassion

After recognizing that everything that has happened was part of God's plan to punish His people, the lamenter turns to God for hope. Great is His faithfulness; He is a savior to those who seek Him. Once justice is served, God will have compassion if they will turn to Him. Then they will not fear, for God will redeem them and judge their enemies.

The siege of Jerusalem

Although Jerusalem was a place of beauty, once the siege began everything changed. Gold was gone, people were cruel, the rich were poor, the white linen of the priest became as black as soot, and some people even ate their children. Fire spread through Zion because the people's uncleanness caused God to abandon them. Enemies came to destroy and Edom rejoiced.

A plea for God's restoration

The final song describes the lack of freedom in their present desperate situation. They had no bread, their women were ravished, and they had no joy because of their sins. The song ends with a strong affirmation of God's eternal rule over all mankind. Since that is true, they can be assured of restoration.

Theological significance

1. It is a fearful and terrible thing to fall into the hands of an angry God. God's wrath justly punishes the sinner.
2. In the midst of trials or divine punishment, there is hope in the faithfulness of God if one repents and seeks His mercy.

Obadiah
Pride goes before a fall

Obadiah lived through the final devastating Babylonian war on Judah (587/86 B.C.) and saw how the people of Judah were taken advantage of by the Edomites. His prophecies were given to encourage the disillusioned Jews who wondered why God did not punish the Edomites for their wicked ways.

Outline of Obadiah

Edom will be judged for its pride	Obad. 1:1-9
Edom's violence against Jerusalem	1:10-14
The day of the Lord for Edom	1:15-21

A further description of how Edom took advantage of the Jews in Jerusalem when the city was destroyed is found in Ezekiel 25, 35, 36, and Psalm 137. Not only did the Edomites mock when Judah fell, they robbed and killed fleeing Jews, tried to make Judah part of their territory, and spoke arrogantly about God.

Edom will be judged for its pride

Edom was very proud because it was easy to defend. To get to the capital, one had to go through a narrow crack between mountains (15 feet wide at points) and then up some fairly steep slopes (1:3,4). Since a major trade route went through the nation, it became very wealthy (1:5) and had many allies (1:7), but God will take all this away when He punishes Edom.

Edom's violence against Jerusalem

A second reason why Edom will be punished is her violence against Jerusalem when it was destroyed by the Babylonians. The Edomites did not help their neighbors, they gloated over Judah's misfortune, helped themselves to whatever the Babylonians did not take, and robbed those who fled to Edom for protection.

The day of the Lord for Edom

The day of the Lord's destruction of Edom is near. Judah will again be holy to God and the Jews will return to inhabit the land (1:17,19-21) but God will destroy Edom and all its people.

Theological significance

1. Pride in military security, wealth, alliance, or wisdom will not save, but will be the source of one's downfall.
2. Gloating over or taking advantage of the misfortunes of others will bring the judgment of God.

Notes

1. T. Overholt, *Threat of Falsehood* (Naperville: Allenson, 1970).
2. R. K. Harrison, *Jeremiah and Lamentations* (Downers Grove: InterVarsity Press, 1973) p. 197.
3. N. K. Gottwald, *Studies in the Book of Lamentations* (London: SCM, 1954) p. 23-32.

Discussion questions

1. Identify God's promises to Jeremiah when he was first called into ministry (Jer. 1). Did he know there would be opposition?
2. In what ways were the people of Judah deceived? How did Jeremiah attempt to transform their understanding?
3. Describe the different ways that Jeremiah reacted to persecution in 11:18-23; 15:15-21; 26:1-19; 38:1-23.
4. What are some similarities and differences between the new (Jer. 31:31-37) and the old covenant under Moses?
5. How does the faithfulness of God give hope in the midst of great sorrow in Lamentations 3?
6. How does the national pride in Edom compare with the pride of countries today?

EXILIC PROPHET

10

Ezekiel
Time of Ministry: 593-571 B.C.

People from Judah were taken into exile in Babylon on three occasions. In 605 B.C., the fourth year of Jehoiakim, Nebuchadnezzar took a small group of Jews to Babylon (including Daniel and his three friends; see Dan. 1:1,2) after his defeat of the Egyptians at Carchemish. A few years later Jehoiakim rebelled against Nebuchadnezzar; consequently the Babylonians attacked Jerusalem and took King Jehoiachin (Jehoiakim had died) and over 10,000 more captives into exile in 597 B.C. (including Ezekiel; see 2 Kings 23:36-24:17; Ezek. 1:2). Zedekiah became the new ruler, but after a few years he also rebelled against Nebuchadnezzar. Jerusalem suffered another attack and was finally destroyed in 587/86 B.C. (2 Kings 24:18-25:21). While Jeremiah proclaimed God's word in Judah during these difficult days, Ezekiel was prophesying to the Jews in Babylonian exile.

Very little is known about the conditions in exile from the book of Ezekiel. This is because Ezekiel was describing to the exiles in Babylon what was happening back in Judah. It seems as though the Babylonians did not persecute Ezekiel for his religion nor did they enslave him. From time to time the elders of Israel gathered together at Ezekiel's house where he would share another word from the Lord (8:1; 14:1; 20:1).

Ezekiel was born during the time of King Josiah (640-609 B.C.). He was married (24:15-18) but there is no indication that he and his wife had any children. He was from a priestly family and was 25 years old when he was deported to Babylon. At age 30 God called him to be a prophet when he saw a vision of the glory of God near the Chebar canal in Babylon (1:1-3). At that time he was filled with the Spirit of God and became dumb, unable to speak except when God opened his mouth (2:1,2; 3:24-27). Ezekiel performed several dramatic sign messages and had a number of visions about what was going on in Jerusalem while he was in Babylon. Some of his messages of judgment counter-acted the optimistic messages of the false prophets who thought that Jerusalem would never be destroyed (4-24). Other messages gave hope to the discouraged exiles after the final destruction of Jerusalem (34-48).

Outline of Ezekiel

Ezekiel's call to prophesy	Ezek. 1-3
God's judgment on Judah	4-24
Signs and messages of Zion's fall	4-7
The glory of God leaves the temple	8-11
Judah's sins will bring destruction	12-24
Oracles of judgment against the nation	25-32
The restoration of Judah	33-48
Hope of restoration and rebirth	33-37
Victory over Gog and Magog	38-39
God's glory in the new temple	40-48

When God spoke to Ezekiel, He frequently used the title "son of man." It is an indication of Ezekiel's humanity which stands in stark contrast to the glory of God. Ezekiel was very aware of the complete holiness and purity of the glorious God he saw in his vision, and very much aware of the terrible sinful acts of the people of Judah. He was God's watchman to warn the nation of His judgment, if they did not repent of their sins.

Ezekiel's call to prophesy

Most of the Jews in exile with Ezekiel thought that God was located in the temple in Jerusalem, so it was quite a surprise to hear that the glory of God was with His people in exile and appeared to Ezekiel. Ezekiel saw a brilliant display of the total otherness of God's splendor. God was on a throne in the midst of a fiery expanse which was moved by winged four-faced heavenly creatures and a series of wheels (1:4-28).[1] After Ezekiel humbled himself in worship, God commissioned him to be a prophet to the stubborn people in exile, not some far away pagan nation which spoke an unintelligible language. Ezekiel was not to fear opposition (they would be like scorpions—2:6) or to be discouraged by their unwillingness to respond positively (2:3-7). He was to declare the Word of God on the scroll he swallowed. If he did not give God's words of warning, He would hold Ezekiel accountable. If he gave the warning and the people refused to listen, then they would be accountable (3:17-21).

God's judgment on Judah

Although most of the people in exile did not believe God would ever allow Jerusalem to be destroyed, Ezekiel used symbolic acts and messages of destruction to convince them that

God would destroy the nation because of its terrible sins. He built a scale model of Jerusalem under military attack (4:1-3) and then laid on his side and ate unclean food to illustrate the terrible conditions in Jerusalem during its siege (4:4-17). The fate of the people was represented by his hair; some were killed by the sword, while others were scattered into many nations (5:1-17). The day of the Lord was near for Jerusalem because their arrogance, abominations, and violence brought God's wrath on them (7:1-27). When this happens, they will know that He is God.

A year after his call, Ezekiel received another vision of the glory of God in the temple at Jerusalem (10:1-21). Many exiles in Babylon believed that Jerusalem would never be destroyed because God Almighty lived in the temple, but in his vision Ezekiel saw the glory of God leave the temple and Jerusalem (9:3; 10:19; 11:22-25). God left because the 70 elders of Judah were worshiping idols in the temple area and in a cellar under the temple (8:5-18). God marked the righteous with a sign, but the wicked were killed and the temple destroyed (9:1-11).[2] The only hope for Judah was for God to remove their sins and give them a new heart (11:14-21).

Ezekiel rejected the false view that God's judgment was a long way off (12:21-28). He condemned the false prophets who misled the people by whitewashing over Judah's problems, saying there would be peace for Jerusalem (13:1-23). This was untrue. If the people did not repent and put away their iniquity, not even the prayers of men of God like Noah, Daniel, or Job could change God's determination to destroy Judah (14:1-23).

In an allegory, Ezekiel compared Judah to a young girl that God cared for and married. But the bride ignored her husband and loved others (foreign customs, idols, her own beauty). Therefore God will judge His adulterous wife, for Judah was worse than her evil sister, the northern nation of Israel, and even worse than Sodom and Gomorrah (16:1-59). This is similar to Ezekiel's parable of the two evil sisters, Oholah (Samaria) and Oholibah (Jerusalem) in chapter 23.

In another allegory, Ezekiel described how a great eagle (Nebuchadnezzar—17:3,12) will control Palestine even though another great eagle (an Egyptian king—17:7,17) will attempt to help Judah. Soon the lion (Judah) will have one of her cubs (King Jehoiachin) captured and taken to Babylon (19:1-9); soon the vine (Judah) will have one of its branches (kings) plucked (19:10-14). Jerusalem will be like a pot over a hot fire and the people will be the meat cooking in it (24:3-5). A final ominous sign was the death of Ezekiel's wife, the desire of his eyes, whom he was not to mourn (24:15-20). God will also destroy His temple, the desire of the people's eyes, and they will be so devastated that they will not be able to mourn (24:20-24). Then they will know that the Lord truly is God.

Although the exile of Judah is sure, one day God will graciously take a tender twig (the Messiah) from the tree and exalt Him (17:22-24). The people will no longer profane God's holy name. Then He will accept them and gather them from exile. Then they will understand that God dealt with them as they deserved (20:39-44).

Throughout all of this section Ezekiel demonstrated that the nation will pay for its sins. Some in exile thought that they were suffering for their father's sins, not their own (18:2). They accused God of being unfair (18:29), but God said that every person will suffer for the sins they themselves commit (18:4-20).

Oracles of judgment on the nations

After a series of brief oracles predicting God's judgment on Ammon, Moab, Edom, and Philistia (25), Ezekiel described God's punishment of the proud and wealthy city of Tyre (27). Ezekiel mockingly lamented this proud king who thought he was a god (28:2,6,11-15) for God will have Nebuchadnezzar destroy him and his wealthy city (26; 28:16-19).[3]

Egypt was also very proud of its rich delta area which was likened to the garden of Eden (29:1-9; 31:1-9). It will become a desert when the Babylonians come and destroy their cities (29:9-30:26). Ezekiel mockingly lamented the pharaoh's death (32:1-8) and pictured Egypt's entrance into Sheol to join the other nations that lie there in shame (32:21-32).

The restoration of Judah

The beginning of Ezekiel's messages of hope and the end of his dumbness coincide with the news that the Babylonians had finally captured the city of Jerusalem (33:21,22). This demoralized those in exile and exposed their false hopes. They began to wonder if there was any hope of returning to Judah and if God would ever fulfill His promises to Abraham and David.

In this new situation Ezekiel was reminded that he is still God's watchman to the exiles (33:1-16). But his message is now a word of hope, because sometime after their judgment God will shepherd His people and gather them together back in the land of Judah. He will make His servant David their messianic prince, restore His covenant of peace with them, give them a new heart, cleanse their iniquity, and bless them with prosperity (34:1-31; 36:22-38; 37:15-28). Then they will know the Lord is God.

God will defeat Judah's enemies, including Edom (a symbol of the rest of the nations) which arrogantly rejoiced when Judah fell and tried to take her land (35:1-36:15). He will also destroy Gog and Magog to sanctify His name, so that all the nations of the earth will recognize that He alone is God (38-39).

The final eight chapters (40-48) contain an unusually detailed description of the measurements for a gigantic temple that would be the center for the restored nation's worship. For the priest Ezekiel, this was a very important aspect of returning to a right relationship with God. The return of the glory of God to this temple was of utmost importance to the completion of God's work (43:1-5). Levitical priests from the family of Zadok will minister in the temple and a prince will rule the people (43:18-44:31). The nation will celebrate its festival at the temple (46) located in the city called "The Lord is there" (48:35). The land will again be divided among the tribes and there will be a fresh water river running from Jerusalem through the Dead Sea and beyond (45:1-8; 47-48).

Theological significance

1. A fresh vision of the splendor of God's glory causes one to bow down, worship, and willingly obey the Word of God.
2. Believers are God's watchmen, called to warn sinners of God's judgment if they do not repent. A watchman who fails to warn will be held accountable by God.
3. God will destroy His own people and their places of worship if they no longer recognize Him or faithfully worship Him.
4. God controls all the nations of the world and will destroy the proud who try to play God.
5. God is just and every person will be held responsible for their own sins.
6. God will keep His promises, cleanse His people's sins, restore them to their land, give them a new heart and covenant, renew true worship, and raise up their Messiah.

The New Testament writers show evidence that they had read the book of Ezekiel. John's description of the glory of God in Revelation 4:1-11 sounds very close to Ezekiel 1 and his swallowing of a scroll in Revelation 10:8-11 is similar to Ezekiel's experience. Jesus and Paul accepted Ezekiel's view of the responsibility of a watchman (Matt. 10:5-15; Acts 18:6; 20:26). Gog and Magog are mentioned again in Revelation 20:8 and the new Jerusalem is part of John's vision (Rev. 21:10,12,16,22).

Notes

1. J. B. Taylor, *Ezekiel* (Downers Grove: InterVarsity Press, 1969), p. 54-59, gives a more detailed description of what Ezekiel saw.
2. Some have suggested that the man in linen in 9:1 was Gabriel or the angel of the Lord, but the text gives no identification.
3. Some believe that the description of the king of Tyre is a picture of the fall of Satan, but the main emphasis is on the historical person who was the king of Tyre. Since the king claimed to be perfect and a god, he was clearly controlled by the lies of Satan and the false mythologies of Tyre's religion.

Discussion questions

1. Is the modern picture of God consistent with Ezekiel's vision or has God sometimes become revisualized or modernized to fit our ideas or wishes?
2. How can God be both the all powerful holy ruler of the world and our loving father?
3. How did Ezekiel correct the people's misunderstanding concerning the possible destruction of the temple, their misunderstanding that they were paying for their fathers' sins, and their doubts about the future fulfillment of God's promises?
4. Is God unconditionally committed to a people or nation that rejects Him? Why or why not?
5. Read some commentaries on Ezekiel and find two or three different ways that people have understood the restoration of the temple in Ezekiel 40-48.
6. How did God's action prove that He was God?

EXILIC PROPHET

11

Daniel
Time of Ministry: 605-535 B.C.

Nebuchadnezzar rose to power in 605 B.C., the year he defeated Egypt, expanding the small nation of Babylon into a world empire. After this battle he went to Jerusalem and took Daniel and his friends into captivity (Dan. 1:1).[1] He returned in 597 B.C. to defeat the Judean king Jehoiachin and take more captives into exile (including Ezekiel). After Zedekiah rebelled, Nebuchadnezzar attacked and totally destroyed Judah in 587/86 B.C. (2 Kings 24-25). Nebuchadnezzar was followed by three relatively weak kings who had short reigns. The last king was Nabonidus (556-539 B.C.), a worshiper of the moon god Sin rather than Marduk. When he spent a number of years away from the capital, he put Belshazzar in charge (Dan. 5).

In 539 B.C. Cyrus, the king of Persia, defeated the Babylonians and established a decree that allowed the Jews to return to Jerusalem (Ezra 1:1-6). About 50,000 Jews returned, but the old man Daniel and many others remained behind in Babylon.

Daniel and his three friends were foreigners and Hebrews from the educated upper class and royal families of Judah (1:3). God preserved His people in captivity through the influence of Daniel who served as one of the top government officials for about 70 years. Although there were some difficult trials along the way, like being thrown into the lion's den, Daniel had a good reputation (5:11-16) and maintained his high position even when the Persians took over after the defeat of the Babylonians.

Daniel's book contains a description of his relationships with government officials and a series of visions about how God rules over all the nations of the earth.

Outline of Daniel

Two literary characteristics make the book of Daniel somewhat unique. Daniel 1:1-2:4a and chapters 8-12 were written in Hebrew like most of the rest of the Old Testament, but 2:4b-7:28 were written in Aramaic, the international language used to conduct political and economic business in that day. This suggests that Daniel wanted parts of his book to be read by non-Hebrew speaking people. A second distinctive is the apocalyptic imagery of strange beasts and plants, symbolic numbers and colors, and detailed predictions about battles and persecution in the future. Although other prophets (especially Zechariah) use symbolism, the visions in Daniel are closer to the apocalyptic imagery in the New Testament book of Revelation than any of the other prophets. When this strange imagery was not interpreted by Daniel, he probably did not feel that that symbol was essential to the overall meaning of the message. Therefore, great care must be taken when modern interpreters attempt to explain what Daniel did not interpret. Even the great and wise prophet Daniel could not understand all the imagery unless it was interpreted by God or an angel (7:16; 8:27; 12:8,9).

God's rule over the Gentile nations

Daniel and his three friends, Shadrach, Meshach, and Abednego, were chosen to enter a three-year educational program in the Babylonian language and its extensive wisdom, religious, and historical literature. Only the best looking and most intelligent young men were brought into this government-sponsored training program for work in the king's court (1:4,5). Daniel and his friends felt that the king's food and wine would defile them (it may have been consecrated to a pagan god), so they diplomatically requested meals of vegetables and water for a 10-day trial. God honored the dedication of these young men and miraculously gave them good health and more wisdom than the other students and 10 times more wisdom than Babylon's wise men (1:17-21).

In the second year of his reign, Nebuchadnezzar had a disturbing dream of a great statue which was destroyed by a rock.

The magicians and wise men of Babylon admitted defeat saying they could not tell the king his dream because a god had not revealed it to them (2:11). Nebuchadnezzar decided to kill the wise men, including Daniel and his friends. After praying for His mercy, God revealed the dream and interpretation to Daniel (2:12-19). Daniel praised God because He has all wisdom and power, and He reveals His mysteries to mankind (2:20-23). Daniel witnessed to the king, revealing that God told him that the head of gold was Nebuchadnezzar (2:28,36-38), the other parts refer to later weaker kingdoms, and the final kingdom was the everlasting kingdom of God (2:44,45). Because he could interpret the dream, Daniel and his God were honored, and his three friends were given new jobs.

Later Nebuchadnezzar made a statue (probably of himself) and required all political officials to bow down to it to demonstrate their loyalty to him (3:1-5). Shadrach, Meshach, and Abed-nego believed that God could deliver them from any harm, so they refused to bow down before the image and were thrown into a blazing furnace. An angelic being from God delivered them unharmed and Nebuchadnezzar was again forced to recognize the power of God (3:24-30).

In spite of this witness to Nebuchadnezzar, he was a very proud man. Finally he was humbled by God and challenged to believe that He was the ruler over all mankind (4:17,25,32). His dream of the destruction of a great tree was fulfilled (4:10-27) and he was humbled and became like a beast (4:28-33). When he was restored to his throne, the king praised, exalted, and honored God, confessing that He was all powerful, true, and just when He humbles the proud and raises up the lowly (4:34-37).

Later while King Nabonidus was away from Babylon, Belshazzar sponsored a great banquet in spite of the fact that the city was at war (5:1-4). At this drunken party, the gold and silver cups from the temple in Jerusalem were desecrated in toasts of praise to the Babylonian gods. In the middle of the party a hand appeared and wrote a message on the palace wall (5:5). No one could read the message except Daniel. It said that God had numbered and weighed Babylon, but found that it did not measure up to His requirements. Therefore God will divide it among the Medes and the Persians (5:25-28). This prophecy was fulfilled that very night in 539 B.C., for that was the night when the Medo-Persian empire defeated Babylon (5:30,31). The fall of Babylon fulfilled the prophecies of Isaiah (13,14) and Jeremiah (50,51) that were given many years earlier.

When the Persians took over the Babylonian empire, they reorganized their vast territory into 120 states (satrapies), with three central commissioners in charge (6:1,2). Daniel was very respected by the king and the most skilled of these officials; therefore, the others tried to find fault with Daniel.[2] Finally they got the king to pass a law that forbade requesting anything from anyone or any god except the king (6:7). When Daniel prayed to God according to his usual custom, he was arrested and thrown into the lion's den. Miraculously God delivered Daniel by sending an angel and closing the mouths of the lions (6:22). The king rejoiced that Daniel was saved and had his enemies thrown into a den of hungry lions.

God's care for His persecuted people

The second half of the book contains more visions of God's sovereign control of the nations, but these messages focus on how God will protect His people in the midst of some very severe persecution. Earlier in the Babylonian reign of Belshazzar, Daniel had a dream (which was very similar to Nebuchadnezzar's dream in chapter 2) about 4 beasts coming from the sea (7:1-8). In this case none of the kings or nations is identified because the focus is entirely on the last beast. The last animal was particularly violent and boastful but finally the Ancient of Days, God Almighty, judged these beasts and gave eternal dominion over all the kingdoms of the earth to the Son of Man (the Messiah) so that all people would serve Him forever (7:9-14). This vision was comforting because it gave assurances that God's saints would inherit the kingdom of God (7:18,27), but it was also very disturbing because it revealed that God's people would go through severe persecution when the last beast and the little horn ruled (7:8,19-25). This small horn is frequently identified with the Antichrist of Revelation 13 and 17.

Two years later Daniel had a similar dream about fighting between a ram, a male goat, and a horn (8:1-8). The ram was interpreted as Medo-Persia (8:20) and the goat represented Greece (8:21) but the violent small horn is not identified. He was some future ruler (8:17,19) who would boast, try to make himself equal to God, and severely persecute the holy people of God for a limited period of time (8:9-14,23-26). Finally he would be defeated by God (8:25). Although this horn is similar to the earlier horn, it is frequently identified with the Greek ruler Antiochus Epiphanes who persecuted and killed many Jews around 165 B.C.[3]

Later in the Persian period, the 80-year-old Daniel was reading in Jeremiah (25:11,12; 29:10) that God would return the people to Jerusalem in 70 years (9:1,2). Suddenly he realized that he had come in 605 B.C. and that it was now 538 B.C., only a few years before they were to return. Daniel fasted and prayed, confessing the nation's sins and recognizing the justice of God in sending them into exile. Then he asked God to turn away His anger and return them to Jerusalem (9:3-19). God told Daniel through the angel Gabriel that it would be 70 weeks of years before God would remove all sin, bring in everlasting righteousness, anoint the holy temple, and fulfill all prophecy (9:24). During this period

Jerusalem would be rebuilt, the anointed Messiah would come and be cut off, and then the city of Jerusalem would be destroyed and the people would undergo great persecution and war (9:25,26). In the middle of the last week of years all worship at the temple would be halted. But by the end of that week, the one who desolated and persecuted the people of God would be defeated.[4] Daniel was extremely alarmed by the description of the war and persecution introduced in chapters 7-9.

The final 3 chapters expand on these themes in order to help future generations to prepare for these trials and to strengthen them with the hope that one day God will reward the faithful with eternal life and the wicked with eternal disgrace (12:1-3).

After three weeks of fasting and praying, Daniel saw a vision of future events from the angel Michael. This report gave Daniel some insight into the unseen spiritual battles going on in his world, for Michael was delayed because of a battle with the evil powers that were controlling Persia (10:1-13,20,21). The angel revealed that there would be four more Persian kings and then the Greeks would defeat them and control all the ancient Near Eastern world (11:1,2). This happened about 200 years later when Alexander the Great defeated the Persians around 331 B.C. His kingdom was later divided into four kingdoms which fought against each other and invaded Palestine, the Beautiful Land. In the midst of these wars a very evil ruler (probably Antiochus Epiphanes) desecrated the temple in Jerusalem, killed many Jews, magnified himself above God, and spoke blasphemies against God (11:29-39). At the end of time, the antichrist will act like this earlier ruler, for he also will blaspheme God (11:36-45). Although this was the the worst persecution that the world had ever known, all the faithful dead have hope for their names are written in God's book of life. They will be resurrected to eternal life, while the wicked will suffer God's judgment (12:1,2). Daniel faithfully wrote down these visions even though he did not totally understand everything they meant or know exactly when these events would take place (12:5-9).

Theological significance

1. All wisdom comes from God. He reveals His wisdom to His faithful servants in order to bring glory to Himself.
2. All power to control individuals and nations rests with God. He raises up whomever he wishes and humbles the proud to demonstrate His power and bring people to submission to Him.
3. Although God's saints have and will suffer great persecution, God will eventually deliver them and give them His eternal kingdom which will be ruled by the Son of Man.

The New Testament contains several references to the book of Daniel. When Jesus was talking about events at the end of time, he reminded them of the persecutions that would happen when the abomination of desolation would be put in the temple at Jerusalem (Matt. 24:15, using Dan. 9:27; 12:11). Revelation 13 refers to several beasts coming out of the sea and focuses on the last one who would blaspheme God and make war against the saints (Dan. 7). Revelation 14 demonstrates that God will judge the beast and deliver the kingdom over to the Son of Man who will come on a cloud (Dan. 7:9-14). Jesus also described (Matt. 24:30; 25:31-46) the Son of Man who would come in His glory, judge the wicked, and raise the righteous dead to life everlasting and the wicked dead to eternal punishment (Dan. 12:1,2).

Notes

1. The apparent inconsistency between Daniel's reference to his going into captivity in the third year of Jehoiakim (Dan. 1:1) after the battle at Carchemish and Jeremiah's association of this event with the fourth year of Jehoiakim is based on either the use of two different calendars (the new year could begin in April or October depending on whether one is using the religious or civil calendar) or the Babylonian practice of not counting the first year of a king's reign as year one, since he had not yet ruled for a year. L. Wood, *A Commentary of Daniel* (Grand Rapids: Zondervan, 1973), p. 25-27.

2. See J. F. Walvoord, *Daniel: The Key to Prophetic Revelation* (Chicago: Moody, 1971), p. 132,33, for a discussion of the identification of the Persian King Darius, mentioned in 5:31; 6:1; 9:1 and 11:1. Many feel this may be the name of one of the Persian generals, others consider it just another name for Cyrus.

3. L. Wood, *A Commentary on Daniel* (Grand Rapids: Zondervan, 1973), p. 214,15.

4. Daniel 9:24-27 is a key passage where millennialists and amillennialists differ. The first group believes these verses are describing events at the end of time just before the millennium. The second group believes these verses are describing events around the time of Christ's first coming and death. See J. F. Walvoord, *Daniel: The Key to Prophetic Revelation* (Chicago: Moody, 1971), p. 216-37, for a discussion of some of these differences.

Discussion questions

1. Compare and contrast the wisdom of Daniel and the Babylonian wise men in Daniel 1 and 2.

2. How were Daniel (chapter 6) and his three friends (chapter 3) examples to those saints who would suffer severe persecution in the future?

3. What was Nebuchadnezzar's and Belshazzar's central sin (chapters 4 and 5)? What was God trying to teach them?

4. How did Daniel's knowledge of Leviticus 26, 1 Kings 8, and Jeremiah 25 influence his prayer in chapter 9?
5. What warnings about interpreting prophecy are provided in 2 Peter 1:20,21? What does 1 Peter 1:10-12 tell us about what the prophets knew and what things they did not know?

POST-EXILIC PROPHETS

12

Haggai, Zechariah, Malachi
Time of Ministry: Haggai 520 B.C.;
Zechariah 520-500 B.C.; Malachi 420 B.C.

Cyrus the king of Persia defeated Babylon in 539 B.C. and decreed that the Hebrews in captivity could return to Palestine and rebuild the temple (Ezra 1:1-3). About 50,000 Jews returned around 538 B.C. under the leadership of the governor Zerubbabel and the high priest Jeshua/Joshua (Ezra 1:11; 2:64-66). Once they returned, the people rebuilt the altar and began to lay the foundation of the temple (Ezra 3:3,8-10). But when the people who lived in the land before the Jews returned tried to join in the rebuilding, Zerubbabel and Jeshua refused to cooperate. In response, they threatened the Jews and caused the work on the temple to stop (Ezra 4:1-5). About 16 years later (520 B.C.), in the second year of the Persian King Darius, God raised up Haggai and Zechariah to challenge the people to start work on the temple again (Ezra 4:24-5:2; Hag. 1:1; Zech. 1:1). The temple was finished four years later, in 516 B.C. (Ezra 6:15).

Later, in 458 B.C., during the reign of the Persian King Artaxerxes, Ezra came to Jerusalem and carried out a religious reform because many people had intermarried with foreigners who worshiped other gods (Ezra 7:1-10; 9:1-10:15). A few years passed and then in 445 B.C. Nehemiah came to Jerusalem to help rebuild the city walls (Neh. 2:1; 6:15). Before long Ezra led another revival because people were intermarrying with foreigners again (Neh. 8:1-10:31). About 25 years after this (420 B.C.), God raised up Malachi to bring the nation back to God because they no longer feared God or lived according to His way.

Haggai
Setting priorities

The rebuilding of the temple was of major concern to the Jews when they first returned to Jerusalem. Since they were continually frustrated on every side by local and Persian authorities, the building of the temple was no longer a priority. Haggai's messages indicate that the people also suffered from an imbalance in their spiritual priorities.

Outline of Haggai

Glorify God and build the temple	Hag. 1:1-15
Comparing the glory of the temple	2:1-9
Holiness precedes blessing	2:10-19
God's work will be accomplished	2:20-23

Haggai was a great motivator. Although he had circumstances, official government policy, economic conditions, and widespread spiritual apathy against him, Haggai was able to overcome these negatives by focusing on the nation's priorities.

Glorify God and build the temple

After years of frustration over not being able to rebuild the temple, most people in Judah just gave up on the idea. They did not have enough money to complete such an expensive project because God sent a drought on their land (1:6,9-11). What income they had, they spent on building nice homes for themselves.[1] Everything pointed to the conclusion that it was not the appropriate time to build the temple (1:4). Haggai challenged these conclusions and set up the higher priorities of doing what God desires and what glorifies Him (1:8). The people revered God, obeyed what He said, and began to work on the temple because they believed that God was with them (1:12-15).

Comparing the glory of the temple

After working on the temple for two months, it was clear that the new temple would be much smaller than Solomon's temple and without gold on the walls, floor, and furniture (2:3; cf. 1 Kings 6:14-36). Many thought that this temple was an embarrassment, not worth the effort. But is exterior beauty what the temple was all about? Haggai challenged the people to set higher priorities, for God's Spirit would strengthen them. He still controls all the nations on the earth and He owns all the gold in the world (2:4-8). In spite of the unimportance of exterior beauty, God gave this new temple great glory when Cyrus paid for the full cost of the temple (Ezra 6:8-10).

Holiness precedes blessing

Two illustrations from the priestly regulations suggest that holiness was not gained by just being in the temple or coming into contact with something holy (2:10-13). Haggai saw that the people were defiled and needed holiness, not just a series of ritualistic observances in the new temple. Once holiness was their priority, they would receive God's blessing (2:14-19).

God's work will be accomplished

Finally Haggai promised the new governor Zerubbabel that God would be with him, would control all the surrounding nations that threatened him, and choose him (a Davidic descendent who would wear the king's ring) to be a sign of God's continuing work to bring about His kingdom on earth (2:20-23).

Theological significance

1. In spite of opposition or negative circumstances, the believer must always give priority to what pleases and glorifies God.
2. Comparisons often lead to discouragement, but God's promises and power give one strength to overcome all problems.
3. God is less concerned about external ritual than He is about internal holiness.

Zechariah
God's restoration of Zion

The prophet Zechariah was probably from a priestly family (Neh. 12:4,16) and he, along with Haggai, played a key role in challenging those who returned from Babylonian captivity to rebuild the temple (Ezra 4:24-5:5). Although the first eight chapters which encouraged the building of the temple are dated around 520-518 B.C., chapters 9-14 have no dates and are more concerned with the time when God will establish His Messianic kingdom. Because of these differences, it is possible that God gave these rather apocalyptic messages in 9-14 a good number of years after the temple was rebuilt.

Outline of Zechariah

Zechariah provided messages of hope for the leaders and a community of believers who were powerless because of their own sinfulness. They were discouraged because it seemed that God was not restoring their nation. To solve these problems, sin must be removed, God's shepherd must be accepted, and then God can establish His kingdom.

Visions to encourage building the temple

Zechariah preceded his visions with a call to repentance (1:1-6). Since God was angry with His people because of their sin, any possible future hope was dependent on their willingness to return to Him. Thankfully, the people repented (1:6).

God gave a series of visions to encourage the people about the restoration of Jerusalem. God was watching over Jerusalem (symbolized by His angels on horses in 1:10,11) and will destroy their enemy nations (symbolized by the horns—1:15, 18-21; 2:8). Jerusalem will be so large that the people returning to it will not fit within its walls. It will be filled with joy, God's presence, and people from many nations (1:16,17; 2:1-7).[2]

The leaders also were encouraged. Joshua the high priest was defended, cleansed, and promised free access to God's throne of grace through prayer. God's eyes would be on the stones of the temple and it would be completed (3:1-10). Through Zerubabel and Joshua (symbolized by the two olive trees), God's Spirit would turn mountains into plains and see to it that the top stone on the temple would soon be in place (4:1-14). God's curse on sin (symbolized by the woman) would be removed (5:1-11) and He would sovereignly control the four corners of the earth (6:1-8). God's promise to send the Branch (the Messiah) was memorialized by a crown of jewels put on Joshua, for the Messiah will have both priestly and kingly functions (6:9-14).

The question of fasting

Some people from the city of Bethel came to Zechariah to find out if they had to continue the fasts that commemorated the burning of the temple in Jerusalem in the fifth month (Jer. 52:12,13), for the new temple was now built. Zechariah questioned whether they were really fasting for God or themselves. Then God challenged them to give priority to practicing justice and compassion and not be stubborn like their fathers (7:8-12). Then God will restore Jerusalem, give them peace, and make Israel a blessing among the nations (8:1-13). God will turn their past fasts into joyous feasts (8:19).

Burdens concerning the future of Israel

The first burdensome message from Zechariah (9-11) described God's judgment of Tyre and Philistia (9:1-7) and His restoration of His people (9:8-11:3). Restoration will include the coming of

Israel's humble king (the Messiah) on a donkey, the renewal of God's covenant relationship with His people, the giving of rain, the removal of all idolatry and false prophecy, and the strengthening of His people. But Israel will reject this king. They will follow the evil shepherd who brings destruction and the good shepherd will be sold for 30 pieces of silver (11:4-17).

The second burdensome message (12-14) described God's deliverance of Judah in a great war against God's people by all the nations of the earth (12:1-9). When God saves Israel and destroys the nations, then the people will recognize the one they pierced, reject their false leaders, mourn their sins, and be cleansed (12:10-13:6). During a final attack on Jerusalem, when many will be killed, God Himself will stand on the Mount of Olives and rescue His people (13:7-14:5). Then He will reign as king over the whole earth and destroy all who refuse to worship Him as the King of Kings (14:9-21).

Theological significance

1. The only way to avoid God's anger is to repent of sins.
2. One day God will judge the wicked among the nations, bring the righteous from the nations to join His people, and dwell among His joyful people.
3. God's work will be accomplished through His Spirit, not by human might, earthly wisdom, or military power.
4. The ritual of fasting is useless if it is not a fast unto God.
5. Although many rejected the good Shepherd from God, through a tremendous demonstration of God's power and grace, one day a multitude of Jews and Gentiles will recognize Him as King of Kings and worship Him.

The New Testament saw that Jesus was the humble king who brought salvation, though He rode on a donkey (Zech. 9:9 and Matt. 21:5). Jesus identified Himself as the good shepherd (Zech. 11:4-14 and John 10:14) and He was sold for 30 pieces of silver (Zech. 11:12 and Matt. 26:15). John 19:37 recognized that the one who was pierced (Zech. 12:10) was Jesus at the cross. Revelation 22:5 talks about a time when there will no longer be any night (see Zech. 14:6,7) and Revelation 22:1,2 refers to the river running out of Jerusalem (Zech. 14:8).

Malachi
Honoring God

The prophet Malachi proclaimed God's word about 100 years after Haggai and Zechariah. The walls of Jerusalem were now up so the city had good security. Since the rebuilding of the temple happened so long ago, many were not very excited about their worship there. The priests were no longer teaching the people about sacrificial regulations. Many were twisting Ezra's command to divorce foreign wives into permission to divorce their Hebrew wives. Some even questioned if there was any value in serving God. Malachi addressed these issues using a dialogue format, which included a series of questions and answers.

Outline of Malachi

Disputation about God's love for Israel	Mal. 1:1-5
Disputation about honoring God in worship	1:6-14
Disputation against the priests	2:1-9
Disputation on marriage and divorce	2:10-16
Disputation on God's justice	2:17-3:6
Disputation on tithing	3:7-12
Disputation on the value of serving God	3:13-4:6

The prophet Malachi believed that there was one essential factor behind the various ethical and worship problems that the people faced. They did not think of God as the great sovereign King who should be feared; therefore, they did not live according to His covenant instructions.

Disputation about God's love for Israel

Although God loved Israel, some of the Jews in Jerusalem questioned whether He really loved them. But proof of God's love is evident in His choice to give His blessings to Jacob rather than Esau (Gen. 25:25,26). God's recent judgment of the Edomite descendants of Esau showed that He did not waver from His plan. Malachi reminded these people that one day God will be glorified around the world, thus encouraging their recommitment to Him.

Disputation about honoring God in worship

God compared Himself to a father and a master, but noted that He did not receive the honor appropriate to such positions. Some questioned this accusation. How did they dishonor God? By offering blind and lame sacrifices that even their own governor would not accept. It would be better to close the temple rather than continue such hypocrisy. People need to remember that He is a great king and His name will be feared among the nations.

Disputation against the priest

God was not worshiped properly because the priests did not act as godly priests by honoring God, giving the people true instruction in God's law, walking in righteousness and peace, or turning people from wickedness. Because they corrupted the Levitical covenant, God will despise and curse them; He will spread the intestinal refuse from the sacrificial animals all over their faces and defile them.

Disputation on marriage and divorce

The Jewish family was defined by its relationship to one father, Abraham, and one God, the God of Israel. But many Hebrews were destroying the traditional family, some by marrying foreign wives and others by divorcing their Hebrew wives. This profaned the people's worship of God at the temple and made it impossible for Him to accept their sacrifices. God hates divorce; certainly anyone who has the Spirit in them would not do this.

Disputation on God's justice

Things were so bad that some actually questioned the justice of God, suggesting that God delights in those who do evil. But God will demonstrate His justice on the earth when He sends His messenger to prepare the way for the coming of the messenger of the covenant (the Messiah).[3] He will purify the Levites and remove the wicked who do not fear God, so that His people will once again present pleasing offerings to God. God is just; His character and His promises do not change.

Disputation on tithing

God asked the people to repent, but they did not seem to know what to repent about. God revealed that they were not tithing. If they would stop robbing God, He would end the plague He had sent to destroy their crops and pour out a blessing so large that they would not have room to store their produce.

Disputation on the value of serving God

Finally, God accused some arrogant people who began to think that it was vain to serve God or to repent. They were so mixed up that they called the proud the blessed ones and the wicked the strong ones. This caused those who feared God to encourage one another by remembering that God has a book which includes the names of those who honor Him. They are God's special possessions, as precious as an only son. In the great day of the Lord, God will distinguish between the wicked and the righteous who serve Him. His burning fire will destroy the arrogant evildoers and give joy and healing to those who fear Him. It pays to remember what God revealed through Moses in the past and what God will do on the day of the Lord when He sends Elijah to restore the nation.

Theological significance

1. God's love and justice do not change. His election and the final judgment on the day of the Lord demonstrate His character.
2. Honoring God, the great King, is not accomplished through hypocritical worship. God deserves our best.

3. God hates divorce and intermarriage with pagans. These acts destroy the family and make worship unacceptable.
4. The teacher/preacher who does not fear God, give true instruction from God's Word, walk in uprightness, and turn people from evil will not receive God's blessing.
5. God does distinguish between the righteous and the wicked; therefore, it is worthwhile to fear and serve God.

In the New Testament book of Romans (9:13) Paul used Malachi 1:2,3—"I loved Jacob, and I hated Esau"—to show that God's purposes were fulfilled by His election of individuals. The messenger who would prepare the way of the Lord in Malachi 3:1 and Elijah in Malachi 4:5 was identified as John the Baptist by Jesus in Matthew 11:9,10,14.

Notes

1. P. A. Verhoef, *The Book of Haggai and Malachi* (Grand Rapids: Eerdmans, 1987), p. 58, believes their houses were furnished with wood paneling on their inner walls, a fairly expensive look which is usually associated with a king's palace (1 Kings 6:15; Jer. 22:14).
2. J. Baldwin, *Haggai, Zechariah, Malachi* (Downers Grove: InterVarsity Press, 1972), p. 109, believes the "me" who was sent against the nation in 2:8 refers to the prophet, but it is likely that the "me" in 2:8 and 2:11 is a reference to the Messiah.
3. Verhoef, *The Book of Haggai and Malachi* (Grand Rapids: Eerdmans, 1987), p. 287-96, sees these verses as eschatological judgments, but part of this prophecy was fulfilled in the first coming of Jesus and part will be fulfilled in His second coming.

Discussion questions

1. What were the three priorities that Haggai emphasized?
2. Why do comparisons often cause discouragement?
3. How did Zechariah encourage the leaders of his day?
4. What prophecies in Zechariah 9-14 relate to the life of Jesus?
5. If people truly honor God, how will this affect their family life, their worship, and their tithing?
6. Why is it worthwhile to fear and serve God?

Bibliography

Psalms

Craigie, P. C. *Psalms 1-50*. Word Biblical Commentary. Waco: Word Books, 1983.

Leupold, H. C. *Exposition of Psalms*. Grand Rapids: Baker Book House, 1969.

Job

Anderson, F. I. *Job*. Tyndale Old Testament Commentaries. Downers Grove: InterVarsity Press, 1976.

Hartley, J. E. *The Book of Job*. New International Commentary on the Old Testament. Grand Rapids: Wm. B. Eerdmans, 1988.

Proverbs

Kidner, D. *The Proverbs*. Tyndale Old Testament Commentaries. Downers Grove: InterVarsity Press, 1964.

Segraves, D. L. *Ancient Wisdom for Today's World*. Hazelwood, MO: Word Afflame Press, 1990.

Ecclesiastes

Kaiser, W. C. *Ecclesiastes: Total Life*. Chicago: Moody Press, 1979.

Kidner, D. *A Time to Mourn and a Time to Dance*. Downers Grove: InterVarsity Press, 1976.

Song of Solomon

Carr, G. L. *Song of Solomon*. Tyndale Old Testament Commentaries. Downers Grove: InterVarsity Press, 1984.

Glickman, S. C. *A Song for Lovers*. Downers Grove: InterVarsity Press, 1976.

Isaiah

Leupold, H. C. *Exposition of Isaiah*. 2 vols. Grand Rapids: Baker Book House, 1968-71.

Ridderbos, J. *Isaiah*. Bible Student's Commentary. Grand Rapids: Zondervan Publishing, 1985.

Jeremiah

Harrison, R. K. *Jeremiah and Lamentations*. Tyndale Old Testament Commentaries. Downers Grove: InterVarsity Press, 1973.

Stedman, R. C. *Expository Studies on Jeremiah: Death of a Nation*. Waco: Word Books, 1976.

Ezekiel

Ellison, H. L. *Ezekiel: The Man and His Message*. Grand Rapids: Wm. B. Eerdmans, 1956.

Taylor, J. B. *Ezekiel*. Tyndale Old Testament Commentaries. Downers Grove: InterVarsity Press, 1969.

Daniel

Baldwin, J. G. *Daniel*. Tyndale Old Testament Commentaries. Downers Grove: InterVarsity Press, 1978.

Walvoord, J. F. *Daniel: The Key to Prophetic Revelation*. Chicago: Moody Press, 1971.

The Minor Prophets

Boice, J. M. *The Minor Prophets*. 2 vols. Grand Rapids: Zondervan Publishing, 1983-86.

Gaebelein, F. C. *The Expositor's Bible Commentary*. Vol. 7. Grand Rapids: Zondervan Publishing, 1986.

Individual Minor Prophets

Baker, D. *Nahum, Habakkuk, Zephaniah*. Tyndale Old Testament Commentaries. Downers Grove: InterVarsity Press, 1988.

Baldwin, J. G. *Haggai, Zechariah, Malachi*. Tyndale Old Testament Commentaries. Downers Grove: InterVarsity Press, 1978.

Hubbard, D. A. *Joel and Amos*. Tyndale Old Testament Commentaries. Downers Grove: InterVarsity Press, 1989.

Kaiser, W. C. *Malachi: God's Unchanging Love*. Grand Rapids: Baker Book House, 1984.